Gerard Condon

D1132282

The Power of Dreams

A CHRISTIAN GUIDE

the columba press

First published in 2008 by
the columba press
55A Spruce Avenue, Stillorgan Industrial Park,
Blackrock, Co Dublin

Cover by Bill Bolger
Illustrations by Andy Devane
The photo of Jung is courtesy of the Kristine Mann Library (New York)
Origination by The Columba Press
Printed in Ireland by ColourBooks Ltd, Dublin

ISBN 978 1 85607 604 3

Acknowledgments
My interest in the spirituality of dreams began in the 1990s at work-
shops conducted at Fordham University by Dr Frederica Halligan. At
the C. G. Jung Centre of New York much hospitality and advice on all
things Jungian was provided by librarians Michele McKee and David
Ward. I am grateful to the community of the Irish College in Rome.
During my time there as Spiritual Director, seminarians often shared
their dreams and I endeavoured to help them find sound interpretations. Those years afforded the opportunity to complete a doctorate on
the theological significance of Jungian dream theory at the Gregorian
University in 2001. I am indebted to the moderator of the study,
Professor Mihály Szentmártoni SJ. Since then I have led seminars on
spiritual dreamwork and facilitated dreamgroups in Rome, Ireland and
New York. The stimulating questions of those who participated have
framed the content of this work. I thank Seán O Boyle of the Columba
Press for his help with editing the text.

Table of Contents

Dedicated to my parents Jack and Helen
for providing a home in which I rested safely
and where, at bedtime, sleep came at once.
(Ps 4:8)

Abbreviations

CW 1-19   C. G. Jung, *The Collected Works of C. G. Jung*, 19
              Volumes. Bollingen Series XX. Edited by W.
              McGuire with translations by R. F. C. Hull
              (New Jersey: Princeton University Press, 1954-
              1979).

The Biblical abbreviations and quotations are from The New
Revised Standard Version, copyright © 1989, by the Division of
Christian Education of the National Council of the Churches of
Christ in the United States of America. Used by permission.

Foundations

Each night during sleep we enter an altered state of consciousness. Our dreams subject us to amazing switches of time and place. We are engaged by terrifying and enchanting emotions. The mind brings out from its storeroom things both old and new (Mt 13:52). In the course of the twentieth century, science, psychology and theology have developed distinct approaches to oneirology, the study of dreams. By following this four week programme you will gain insight from these disciplines and learn to see a spiritual dimension in your dreams.

Psychology provides the most comprehensive framework for the study of dreams. Today's spiritual dreamwork is largely inspired by the Swiss psychologist Carl Gustav Jung (1875-1961). In opposition to his erstwhile mentor Sigmund Freud (1856-1939), Jung asserted that spirituality is essential for mental health. He retrieved an ancient tradition that, in some cases, 'dreams are sent by God'.[1]

The notion that God can communicate with human beings in dreams is clearly affirmed in the Bible and Christian tradition. Jacob's dream of a ladder connecting heaven and earth is exemplary:

Taking one of the stones of the place,
he put it under his head and lay down.
And he dreamed there was a ladder set up on the earth,
the top of it reaching to heaven. ...
And the Lord stood beside him and said,...
'Know that I am with you

---

1. 'Somnia a Deo missa.' C. G. Jung, *Symbols and the Interpretation of Dreams*, (1961) CW 18, par. 437. The phrase is attributed to Macrobius, a fifth century AD Roman author.

and will keep you wherever you go.' ...
Then Jacob woke from his sleep and said,
'Surely the Lord is in this place – and I did not know it! ...
How awesome is this place!
This is none other than the house of God,
and this is the gate of heaven.'
So Jacob rose early in the morning,
he took the stone that he had put under his head,
and set it up for a pillar and poured oil on the top of it.
(Gen 28:11-18)

Jacob had the dream at a time of rivalry with his brother Esau to win the favour of their father, Isaac. The experience resonated with the awe-inspiring numinosity of a divine encounter. It assured him of God's support. Next day Jacob took the stone he had used for a pillow and set it up as a shrine. He called the place Bethel (Gen 28:19), which means 'the house of God'. Much to his surprise, Jacob considered the dream itself a sanctuary, a dwelling place for the divine.

Among the earliest recorded dreams in Christian tradition are those of St Perpetua prior to her martyrdom on March 7, 203.[2] This account describes dreaming as a charism, a gift of the Spirit. In one dream, Perpetua, like Jacob, sees a ladder leading to heaven. It injures those mounting it that do not keep looking upwards. Perpetua imagined herself and her fellow Christian prisoners steadfastly climbing the ladder. She awoke comforted by the insight that she could and would remain strong in her faith.

A theology of dreams is found in several ancient Christian writers. Tertullian (160-220), the first Latin-based theologian, went so far as to state that 'the majority of people derive their knowledge of God through dreams.'[3] Bishop Synesius of Cyrene (c.370-c.414) wrote *On Sleep*, a substantial treatise on dreamwork and its role in the spiritual life. More than a millennium later, Jerónimo Gracián (1545-1614), the confessor of St Teresa of

---

2. *Passio Sanctarum Perpetuae et Felicitatis*, 3-10.
3. '... et maior paene vis hominum ex visionibus deum discunt.' Tertullian, *De Anima*, 47.2.

Ávila, listed dreams as the tenth in his twelve ways of the Holy Spirit.

The decline of theological reflection on dreams began in the late Middle Ages as Christian spirituality came to be identified with official dogmas and practices accessed through the use of reason. Dreams were viewed as being too personal and irrational to be sources for an orthodox spirituality. Christian theology focuses on the Christ event as the origin and summit of all revelation about God. It benchmarks any personal spiritual insights, such as those gained from dreams, against the revelation of God in Jesus.

Today, the secular disciplines of science and psychology have replaced theology as the dominant forums for discussing dreams. Yet many people want to look at their dreams through the lens of spirituality. The dream, like religion, is a source of guidance and a gateway to mystery. Spiritual dreamwork is particularly encouraged in that broad church known as the New Age. My aim is to retrieve a sense of the religious relevance of dreams for mainstream Christianity.

'We are,' as Shakespeare put it, 'such stuff as dreams are made on, and our little life is rounded with a sleep.'[4] Dreams engage us on wavelengths far broader than the rational language which dominates theology. In our technological age, people yearn for moments of personal encounter with the divine. Experiencing God has become as important as understanding God. Dreamwork promotes that sense of wonder and personal identity which is foundational for a relationship with the divine. Reaching out to God paradoxically requires us to look into the depths of ourselves. In coming closer to the truth about yourself, you will also find yourself standing more closely with Christ before the Father.

From these comments it should be clear that the spirituality of dreams does not involve seeking out spectacular nocturnal apparitions. Christian dreamwork is more to do with ourselves than God. It is based on the claim that God's Spirit is evident in our unconscious dreams as well as our conscious thoughts. Dreamwork gives a larger picture of the personality than that

---

4. W. Shakespeare, *The Tempest*, act 4, scene 1.156-158.

offered by waking life alone. Its aim is to make us more completely disposed to the mutual truths of personal existence and God's quietly insistent presence in our lives.

Professional and Non-Professional Dreamwork

The study of dreams has developed in three distinct ways over the past one hundred and fifty years.[5] Nineteenth century dreamwork, influenced by the Enlightenment, consisted largely of scientific observation. At the same time, the Romantic reaction against science initiated an artistic approach to dream analysis. This was foundational to the psychological methods of Freud and Jung. In the past fifty years new medical technology has revived the scientific approach. Most recently a movement for the democratisation of dream analysis has emerged. An appreciation for the dreamwork conducted in traditional cultures coupled with the emergence of dreamgroups has promoted the use of dreams in a public setting outside the therapist's studio and the sleep laboratory. The present work belongs to this emerging perspective.

Advocates of non-professional dreamwork advise caution. A formal qualification in psychology is a better foundation for dream interpretation than commonsense. Our method uses insights from psychology; however, like a little bit of surgery, such selective reading can be misleading. Amateur dreamwork tends to make premature and facile interpretations. A professional analyst is more likely to see the dream objectively and make reliable connections with the personal and cultural context of the dreamer. In personal dreamwork, the possibility of achieving accurate insight is reduced by a resistance to the generally compensatory message of the dream. In other words, our desire to avoid the challenging truth posed by a dream, may lead to a distortion of its message. Furthermore, the stimulation of the unconscious by dream analysis poses some risk of mental disturbance, something which only the professionally trained therapist can manage. Non-professional dreamwork is only appropriate for individuals with normal mental functioning.

---

5. S. Shamdasani, *Jung and the Making of Modern Psychology. The Dream of a Science* (Cambridge University Press, 2003), 159-162.

The strategy suggested here is a matter of dream appreciation. We do not aim to analyse ourselves or others in a psychotherapeutic fashion. Jung held that dreams are carefully phrased and relatively transparent messages from the unconscious. Our approach conceives dreamwork as a gateway to a more considered life and a more comprehensive sense of our place in the world. This should enhance rather than threaten mental health. However, the wisdom of limiting dreamwork should be noted. Waking thoughts and decisions are the foundation for responsible living. The Bible warns that dreams can provoke idle worrying or a desire to have knowledge that is reserved to God alone (Deut 13:1-5; Eccl 5:3; Sir 40:5). Theologians from Tertullian to Thomas Aquinas have stated that in dreams the sleeper is sensitive to the voices of demons as well as angels. A Christian approaches the chaotic world of the unconscious with caution and judges the fruits of dreamwork in the light of the gospel.

How to use this programme
This programme provides insights into the science, psychology, theology and spirituality of dreams for each day of a lunar cycle. Set aside a few minutes at a regular time each day to study the assigned input. While each of the daily readings is self-contained, the themes chosen are given in logical succession and are intended to cumulatively contribute to your knowledge, understanding and skills concerning dreams and dreamwork.

You are also invited to begin a personal journal or make additional use of an existing journal. Narrating and writing about your own dreams will best illustrate the principles outlined in the readings. Continue or begin to write about your everyday experience, as dreams are generally a response to your conscious life. You might also react to the assigned reading from this book. To this end a reflection question or activity for each day is suggested in Appendix A.

On awakening each morning try to remember a few key images from a dream of the previous night on a note-pad at your bedside. Later that day use these notes to write out the full dream story in your journal. Out of respect for the dream, it should simply be an objective account and avoid interpretation. Still later set aside some space in your journal to record an analysis of the dream. In your analysis, pay particular attention to the feelings evoked by the images, because dreams frequently portray emotions in picture-form. Also note your personal and cultural associations with the key images. Ask yourself in relation to each element of the dream: 'What does this represent for me?' The people and objects in dreams usually embody aspects of the dreamer's own personality.

Dreams are normally quite difficult to remember. However, the decision to follow this course will undoubtedly improve your dream recall. Do not be surprised if you have one or two really significant dreams during the next month. Jung noticed that spectacular dreams sometimes occur at the beginning of dreamwork.[6] Such dreams outline a grand vision of your life that will provide key insights into its meaning. So called initial dreams tend to be transparent in meaning in contrast with the obscurity of many others.

The Dreamgroup

This book can be used with others in a dreamgroup. Each member of the group agrees to follow the programme day-by-day, while the weekly meeting provides a forum for the sharing of insights and dreamwork. The dreamgroup is a non-professional forum. It should have the friendly atmosphere of storytelling at a family gathering rather than the serious tone of group psychotherapy. The leader is responsible for the formation of the group and efficient running of the meetings. His or her role is enhanced by background knowledge of oneirology.

Participation in a dreamgroup stimulates dream recall and gives practice in the skill of dream analysis. It fosters accountability in the discipline of examining one's dreams. The circumspect language of dreams facilitates self-disclosure in a safe and oftentimes humorous way. The exercise builds strong ties of community as dreams concern those fundamental joys and sorrows where we all find common ground.

When conducted in the context of a faith community such as a parish or theology institute, spiritually themed dreams are likely to be contributed. Many of the insights provided in this

6. C. G. Jung, 'The Practical Use of Dream-Analysis' (1934) CW 16, pars. 296, 313, 343.

book will make for discussions based on the Bible and Christian tradition. The meetings could well begin or end with some time in prayer. Exemplary vocal prayers are given in Appendix B. Jesus of Nazareth frequently brought people to new life simply by gathering them together in innovative ways (Lk 5:29-32; 7:36-50; 8:19-21; 14:7-24). Group dreamwork may provide one such forum for spiritual growth today.

Ideally the dreamgroup should be made up of six to nine people and meet on each occasion for sixty to eighty minutes to discuss a dream presented by one or two members, depending on the size of the group. Before the dreamwork, the leader can facilitate discussion on the previous week's readings from this book and offer some additional insights from his/her own background reading. Then a dream is shared by one of the members according to the ground rules and procedure outlined in Appendix C. When two members have agreed to contribute a dream, the leader might briefly preview the following week's readings in an interval between the two cases. In most dreamgroups the leader does not contribute a personal dream so as to preserve his/her role as a facilitator throughout the programme.

I suggest that the dreamgroup meet on five occasions as follows:

Meeting 1: Orientation Meeting

The leader distributes this book to the group, explains the procedure of the meetings and reviews this introduction. A sample dream from an anonymous source is provided by the leader and analysed according to the method in Appendix C. At the end of this and each of the following gatherings, one or two members pledge to share an upcoming dream at the next encounter.

Meeting 2: At the Conclusion of Week One

Most of the readings for the first week concern scientific findings about sleep. Participants might share their own experiences of sleep hygiene issues and their ability to manage dream retrieval. Days 5 and 6 are based on a Jungian approach to remembering the dream and telling its story in a dedicated dream log. The final input for the week links the ability to fall asleep with religious faith.

Meeting 3: At the Conclusion of Week Two

In the readings of the second week the key insights of psychology on the nature, function and interpretation of dreams are summarised. An introduction to Sigmund Freud's theory of dreams is provided on Day 1. All subsequent inputs are based on Jung's approach to oneirology. The leader might prepare some additional information or illustrations on the life and times of Carl Jung.

Meeting 4: At the Conclusion of Week Three

The readings of the third week are theological reflections on the question of dreams as a vehicle for God's presence. The perspectives found in the Bible and Christian tradition are summarised. The leader might use the Bible to elaborate some of the scriptural references included.

Meeting 5: At the Conclusion of Week Four

The final meeting reviews the spirituality of dreamwork. The focus here is on putting dreamwork at the service of religious living. The programme examines the potential of dreams for determining your 'myth' or 'personal vocation' from God. Members might also share any inklings of their own 'myth'. The last event of the programme could well conclude with some celebratory refreshments.

* * *

The theological method of this programme is inductive. We begin with the human experience of sleeping and dreaming and look therein for traces of God's presence. Much of the Reformed or Protestant tradition has been deductive, beginning from revelation about God in the Bible and setting the natural and supernatural orders in a confrontational dialogue. The Catholic imagination, on the other hand, thinks that 'the very commonness of everyday things harbours the eternal marvel and silent mystery of God and his grace.'[7] Following this model, dreams can be considered among the countless opportunities for contemplating the Creator that fill creation.

From an inductive perspective the science and psychology of dreams constitutes a legitimate starting point for theological

7. K. Rahner, *Belief Today* (New York: Sheed and Ward, 1967), 14.

reflection on the subject. Science, to paraphrase Albert Einstein, is lame without religion. The science of psychology, and in particular Jungian psychology, has a profound sympathy for the religious instinct. However, scientific disciplines are essentially not well disposed to a Christian reading of dreams. They remain focused on what is natural and cannot fully engage with the supernatural images of God which Christians derive from Jesus. It is not surprising that Jung's psychology of religion, because it is based on human experience more than divine revelation, contains many elements that are contrary to Christian doctrine.

I have adopted the dispensation given to the people of Israel and since used by all theologians who are inductive in outlook. God allowed the Hebrews to plunder gold from pagan Egypt as they set out on the journey to the Promised Land (Ex 11:2; 12:35-36). Similarly, this study uses insights from science and psychology in an *aggiornamento* (updating) of the ancient Christian respect for dreams. Not only are we looking for spiritual jewels in the natural sciences, but bringing the light of the gospel to bear on the chaotic world of the dream.

This is in keeping with an important principle of Christian theology which states that divine grace does not destroy nature but makes it perfect.[8] Christianity seeks not to radically alter creation, but recognise its innate potential and bring about its fulfillment. We are already made in God's image, but we can still grow in divine likeness (Gen 1:26). May this month's dreamwork advance God's vision in you.

---

8. 'Gratia non tollit naturam sed perficit eam.' T. Aquinas, *Summa Theologica* I.8 and 2.

Science

You will not fear the terror of the night. Ps 91:5

Day 1: Getting to Sleep

The *Encyclopedia Britannica* defines sleep as a 'normal, easily reversible, recurrent and spontaneous state of decreased and less efficient responsiveness to external stimulation.'[1] It is a basic human need. Signs of sleepiness include yawning, stretching and a drooping of the eyelids. After eighteen hours of wakefulness the average adult strongly feels the need to be asleep. Reaction time slows, much as if alcohol has been consumed. Unexpected *microsleeps* begin to occur, whereby the train of thought is momentarily lost.[2] After twenty four hours of being awake the need for sleep becomes overwhelming. The record for the longest period of continuous wakefulness in a sleep laboratory setting is held by Randy Gardner of San Diego who remained awake for 264 hours in December 1963.

The Stanford Sleepiness Scale is a self-rated instrument which indicates the degree of tiredness averaged over one hour. What number are you at the moment?

1	=	Feeling active and vital
2	=	Functioning at high level and able to concentrate
3	=	Relaxed and responsive
4	=	A little foggy, not functioning at peak
5	=	Beginning to lose interest in staying awake
6	=	Fighting sleep, would prefer to lie down
7	=	Reverie, struggling to remain awake

1. D. Foulkes, W. B. Webb, R. D. Cartwright, 'Sleep and Dreams' in *Encyclopaedia Britannica* 27 (Chicago: Chicago University Press, 1991), 298.
2. Full descriptions of the technical terms given in italics during this week are in M. Carskadon (ed), *Encyclopedia of Sleep and Dreaming* (New York: Macmillan, 1993).

The onset of sleep is usually effortless when a person is physically tired, mentally relaxed and in a comfortable bed free of distraction. Sleep naturally occurs in harmony with the *circadian rhythm*, an internal clock that effects a twenty-four hour cycle of fluctuation in body temperature, urine production and blood pressure. This biological timekeeper facilitates sleep in the evening and alertness in the morning. In laboratory experiments, where subjects are held in complete isolation from external indicators, a cycle of rest-activity consistent with night-time and daytime still persists. However most of the time signals (*Zeitgebers*) for the circadian rhythm are derived from the environment and especially the succession of light and darkness.

The circadian clock is about one hour slow in evening types or 'night owls' while it runs a little faster for morning types. A variation of the rhythm known as *Delayed Sleep Phase Syndrome* prevents the natural onset of sleep until around 3.00 am and makes it difficult to awaken before mid-day. This typically occurs in adolescence and young adulthood. The corollary condition, *Advanced Sleep Phase Syndrome*, is more common in the elderly. It is identified by an overwhelming sleepiness in the early evening with awakening at 3.00 or 4.00 am.

Today's world provides significant disruptions to the natural tendency towards daytime alertness and night-time sleepiness. The existence of electricity is a crucial factor in being able to achieve a '24/7' lifestyle. However, night workers are prone to sleepiness during work and generally do not get adequate sleep. Evening types are more adapted to nocturnal working hours. The use of daylight levels of artificial light at night shift-work and total darkness during daytime sleep can somewhat compensate for the disruption to the circadian pattern.

Jet lag involves a short term circadian rhythm disruption which lasts until the biological clock catches up with its new environment. It is most evident in eastwards travel which goes against the direction of the circadian clock. To allay the discomfort, it is recommended that a person begin to adjust from a home-based to a destination-based schedule a day or so before travel. On arrival the local day-night cycle should be adopted as soon as possible.

Insomnia is the experience of regularly having difficulty

falling or staying asleep. It is the most frequent sleep disorder affecting up to twenty percent of the population each year for one to two weeks. However the condition tends to be over-reported, since people usually get more sleep than they realise. Insomnia results in fatigue and irritability during the day. Insomniacs are found to have higher levels of depression, physical pain and stress than the general population. These factors may explain the causes of insomnia and point to the focus of primary treatment. The anxiety of not being able to fall asleep can itself contribute to sleeplessness.

For people with adequate mental and physical health, fidelity to the following sleep hygiene practices promotes normal sleep patterns:

- Have a regular bedtime. Spend about thirty minutes 'winding down' before going to bed. This serves to relax the body and signals the mind that sleep-time is approaching.
- Foods that are high in L-Tryptophan are conducive to sleep. These include milk and milk based products, as well as turkey, rice and peanuts. This amino acid is a precursor to serotonin, a sedative chemical in the brain.
- Low levels of light in the environment before bedtime stimulates the production of the hormone melatonin. This also has a calming and sleep-inducing effect.
- Limit napping. A short nap after lunch is invigorating. However, too much sleep during the day reduces the significance of the night sleep. Excessive napping can create a harmful cycle of night sleeplessness, followed by a tendency to sleep by day.
- Restrict the time for sleep. For the average adult seven and a half hours is the optimal length of sleep. If your sleep is too long, it will be lighter and more disturbed. A consolidated sleep time makes sleep deeper.
- Daytime exercise promotes sleep onset by creating physical fatigue.
- Early morning exposure to light will advance the biological clock, leading to drowsiness by evening.
- Restrict caffeine and other stimulants. Afternoon or night-time consumption of caffeine or nicotine typically prevents sleep onset.

- Have a peaceful bedroom. Insomniacs are often found to have cues for being awake (TV, telephone, food) rather than asleep in their bedroom.
- Do not wait in bed for sleep. After ten to twenty minutes, get up and go to another room to sit quietly and read or listen to some gentle music. Go back to bed when you are sleepy. Returning to a cooler bed will also promote sleep as a small reduction in body temperature is a precursor to sleep.
- Be relaxed in mind. Extreme joys and sorrows prevent the onset of sleep. In the time before sleep engage in some journaling or quiet conversation with a friend so as to purge your anxieties.
- Forget yourself. Telling bedtime stories to children or even counting sheep were all intended to move mental attention away from oneself. Some light reading in bed can also effect a distraction and so facilitate the 'letting go' of sleep.

Day 2: The Architecture of Sleep

Twentieth century sleep research was revolutionised by the development of the *electroencephalogram* (EEG), an instrument which produces a graph of the electrical activity of the brain. Characteristic patterns of the brain's activity such as sleeping, a coma or an epileptic seizure can be recognised by this apparatus. Using a specially adapted EEG at their sleep laboratory in Chicago during the 1950s, Aserinsky, Kleitman and Dement identified dreaming as a distinct part of an elaborate sleep cycle.

Sleep is essentially a state of reduced alertness. The process of going to sleep is often accompanied by simple mental images of descent, literally of 'falling asleep.' The senses gradually become less connected to external reality and the ability to direct thought diminishes. This transitional period is sometimes characterised by involuntary muscular spasms (known as *hypnagogic jerks*) whereby the conscious mind momentarily resists its diminishing self-control. It is followed by four successively deeper stages of sleep. These together last up to ninety minutes and are distinguished by a progressive decrease in the frequency of brain waves and the rates of pulse and respiration.

In the average adult, Stage One sleep lasts just a few minutes and can easily be disturbed. In addition to characteristic EEG wave patterns it is identified by a slow rolling movement of the eyeball. Stage Two sleep is distinguished by its EEG pattern alone and has no physical characteristics apart from a higher arousal threshold. Stage Three sleep is marked by slower EEG brain waves, the absence of eye movement and a further deepening of sleep. Stage Four sleep is also characterised by slow waves on the EEG and the person is most deeply asleep. Stage Three and Four sleep are often grouped under the umbrella term *slow wave sleep*. This type is especially evident in the sleep of children and young adults and less so in the elderly. In other words, the depth of sleep is reduced with aging.

At the conclusion of Stage Four sleep the body turns and the depth of sleep gradually lessens through Stages Three and Two. With the recurrence of Stage One, *Rapid Eye Movement* (REM) sleep begins. The closed eyes show bursts of rapid darting movement beneath the eyelids as distinct from the slow rolling motion of Stage One sleep. During REM sleep the brain's electrical activity assumes a similar pattern to being awake. The pulse quickens, there is greater variability in breathing. The physiology of sexual arousal occurs. REM is accompanied by the greatest lessening of muscle tone during the entire sleep cycle. Muscular activity is almost suspended even though the sleeper is effectively awake in other respects. For this reason the REM period is sometimes labelled *paradoxical sleep*.

The scientific research linked REM sleep to dreams. It was originally hypothesised by Dement that the eye movement of REM is synchronous with the visual imagery of the dream. There is a high probability that a sleeper awakened during REM will report having been in a dream. Sleep laboratory experiments showed that people awoken in Stage One-Four sleep also report mental activity, but this generally lacks the narrative quality of a proper dream. However other research casts doubt on Dement's theory. For example, REM is also observable in the dreams of the congenitally blind whose dreams lack visual imagery.

In a sleep period lasting six to nine hours, four to six sleep cycles of ninety minutes can be anticipated. REM normally makes up twenty to twenty-five percent of adult sleep. Over the course of a night's sleep the time spent in Stage Three and Four Sleep decreases while the time dedicated to REM in each cycle proportionally increases. The length of dreams increases from about ten minutes to about twenty five minutes per cycle as the night progresses. In an average night's sleep of seven and a half hours about five dreams totalling ninety minutes can be anticipated.

Scientific studies have shown that REM or dream sleep is necessary for mental health. Whereas the deprivation of non-dream sleep results in physical tiredness, the loss of REM sleep makes people anxious, irritable and less capable of problem solving the following day. Those completely deprived of REM for an extended time tend to entertain dream-like fantasies when awake. This may explain the incidence of *delirium tremens* in alcoholics as alcohol consumption effects a reduction of REM sleep. As a result of ongoing REM deprivation dreams may, in compensation, erupt into the waking life of an alcoholic. Research has further demonstrated a 'REM rebound effect' whereby a REM sleep deficit is recovered in subsequent nights' sleep. Finally, the discovery that REM sleep accounts for half of infant sleep, but just one-fifth of sleep in the elderly, suggests that dreaming plays a role in socialisation. Dreams help identify our place in the world and this need is more urgent in the young.

The transition from sleep to wakefulness is not instant-aneous. A majority of adults in Western society rely on alarm clocks to awaken at the desired time. The loudness and mean-ingfulness of a sound determines its ability to arouse. A mother may hear the cry of her child, but sleep through a louder envir-onmental noise that evokes no personal response. The circadian rhythm includes a sleep terminator, principally through a rise in body temperature. Self-suggesting the time of awakening prior to sleep is a partly effective means of waking up at that time.

Animals have patterns of sleep resembling those of human beings. Large and long-living animals generally need less rest. The elephant sleeps for only four hours a day, mostly while standing. By contrast, small and short lived animals such as the hamster sleep for fourteen hours. This may be because small mammals have little fat reserves and their sleep functions for energy conservation.

Water bound animals such as the dolphin sleep while swim-ming, resting half the brain at a time. The active hemisphere of the brain controls breathing and one eye keeps watch for dan-ger. Birds have been shown to exhibit patterns of quiet sleep fol-lowed by active sleep that is analogous to non-REM and REM. Their sleep is also unihemispheric. Fish exhibit patterns of sleep-like behaviour alternated with activity. However, evidence of slow wave or REM sleep in fish has not been established. Even insects exhibit regular cycles of activity followed by rest when responsiveness to external stimuli is reduced. There is a debate as to whether reptiles actually sleep. Like warm blooded animals they show decreased alertness at times. However, their brain activity does not show the characteristic cyclical patterns of slow wave sleep followed by REM.

REM can be readily measured and observed in the sleep of some animals. While just twelve percent of a rabbit's sleep is spent in REM, some thirty percent of a dog's sleep has characteristic REM patterns. The observer of a sleeping dog will note many characteristics of dream sleep such as irregular breathing and passing enactments of the dream imagery. Animals that are born helpless (dogs and cats) have more REM sleep than those born in a developed state (horse, giraffe), demonstrating the role of dreams in socialisation. However, even with this evidence, it cannot be assumed that animals dream, since they cannot communicate the experience to us.

Day 3:
Yawning, Snoring and Other Terrors of the Night

Yawning is an involuntary gaping of the mouth that begins with a slow intake of breath and ends with a shorter exhalation. It is a feature of all animal life. Most yawning occurs in preparation for sleep or after waking and is often accompanied by stretching. Yawning is frequently a sign of being bored. It may be a valiant attempt by the mind to maintain a state of alertness. However, the theory that yawning is the body's attempt to increase its level of oxygen in the blood cannot be upheld scientifically. Within a group, yawning typically signals a person's intention of going to bed. Yawning is a highly contagious activity. Indeed simply reading this paragraph may precipitate a bout of yawning!

Snoring is produced by the vibration of soft tissue in the throat. The relaxation of the muscles during sleep reduces the strength of the palate which causes the noisy vibration while breathing. Among the contributory factors are obesity (due to the increased size of the throat tissue) and breathing through the mouth. Snoring is more common among men, especially those aged over thirty-five. Some research indicates that people who snore a lot are at greater risk of heart disease. Sleeping on one's side is generally thought to reduce the incidence of snoring. In severe cases a surgical procedure to enlarge the airway can help.

Apnea is the temporary cessation of breathing during sleep that is effectively an extended pause between breaths. It is often associated with snoring. In many cases it is provoked by obstructed airways. So called 'obstructive apnea' is sometimes linked to obesity and heart disease. Its most severe form is as a temporary failure of breathing without obstruction. An episode of apnea often leads to a brief awakening. In severe cases sufferers complain of morning headaches which can be attributed to lower-than-normal levels of oxygen in the blood.

Somniloquy or sleep-talking involves vocalisations during sleep. These are usually difficult to comprehend. Sleep-talking occurs somewhat more frequently in REM than non-REM sleep. This indicates an explanation of the event as the acting out of a dream.

Incidents of *somnambulism* or sleep-walking occur in up to forty percent of children, especially in those aged eleven to twelve. It tends to happen during non-REM sleep, disproving the hypothesis that the event is a dream enactment. Sleep-walking can range from simply sitting up in the bed and mumbling incoherently to actually leaving the house. The person's eyes are open, but do not appear focused. During an episode the sleep-walker is aware of his or her surroundings and will usually be able to avoid obstacles. It is best to gently guide the sleepwalker back to bed. Somnambulism does not indicate an underlying psychiatric condition.

Another sleeping condition associated with childhood is enuresis or *bed-wetting*. It regularly occurs in the sleep of twenty-five per cent of four year olds and is not uncommon up to young adulthood. The likely causes include abnormalities in the urinary system, delayed psychological maturity and day-time stresses. Punitive responses from parents are not an effective remedy. Instead the underlying factors should be identified and treated. Positively reassuring the child also encourages a growing out of the condition.

Episodes of bruxism or *tooth-grinding* regularly occur in the sleep of most people. The event is strongly associated with day-time stress. It becomes a medical problem when there is excessive tooth wear or jaw pain. Incidence of the issue can be reduced by resolving the causes of stress. In severe cases the use of a plastic bite splint is also effective.

Narcolepsy is an involuntary tendency to fall asleep during the day. The term literally means 'sleep seizure' and can afflict a person several times a day. Less than one per cent of the population is affected by this disorder. Laboratory tests link episodes of the condition to REM sleep. It has three key forms: *Cataplexy* is distinguished by short episodes of loss in muscle tone. *Sleep paralysis* is an inability to move or speak at the beginning or end of a regular night's sleep. *Hypnagogic hallucinations* are visions that vividly engage all five senses.

The *pavor nocturnus* or *night-terror* occurs most frequently in children. It usually happens in Stage Four sleep, about two hours after the onset of sleep. The event is often accompanied by frantic shrieking and flailing of the arms and a rise in heart-rate and respiration. The sufferer can feel disoriented and take some time to regain composure. The night terror generally yields minimal recall of its mental content. The victim sometimes describes feeling choked or the sensation of being crushed. In Psalm 91, the poet professes faith in a God who can deliver us from the terrors of the night (Ps 91:5).

The night terror is to be distinguished from the *nightmare*. Whereas the night-terror occurs during slow wave sleep, nightmares are associated with REM and essentially involve a frightening dream. Following a nightmare, the dreamer is able to recall an awful experience which normally concludes with the person being in great danger. Children generally feel threatened by monstrous animals or machines, whereas adult nightmares usually involve danger from other people. Nightmares, like all other dreams, represent a person's unconscious memories, problems, wishes and fears using emotion-laden imagery. The frequency of these bad dreams tends to decrease with age. Some studies report that sensitive people are more likely to have nightmares. Times of stress also increases their frequency. Finally, a traumatic event in waking life can provide the content of the nightmare.

Do the deaf hear and the blind see in their dreams? Some dreams have an auditory dimension, in the sense of the person being addressed by the other characters of the dream. A disembodied voice is a feature of other dreams. In dreams our senses are generally limited to those available in waking life. Thus the dreams of the congenitally deaf do not possess an auditory quality. Likewise, those who are blind since birth report no experience of seeing in their dreams. Instead, the dreams of the congenitally blind employ the language of the other four senses. Their dreams have a sense of location and movement but not of sight. On the other hand, those who become blind or deaf during life continue to have dreams involving vision and hearing.

Most dreams recalled from REM sleep are in colour. Images from non-REM sleep tend to be less vivid. A small number of people describe their dreams in monochrome. From the viewpoint of psychology, the colour itself may represent the dream message. The presence of yellow in a dream might be interpreted as the dreamer's cowardice. Grey might reflect the subject's bored or drab attitude to life. White alludes to purity. In general dream images are depicted in darker tones than in real life. This fact is interpreted by psychologists as the dream's ability to represent the unknown and the unconscious. Like the dark earth or the depths of the ocean, the obscurity of the dream's setting may feel threatening, but can also be viewed as a place for exploration and a source of new life.

Day 4: Why do we Sleep and Dream?

Scientific research indicates that sleep serves two functions. Firstly, it is an adaptation to our environment. Each species finds a sleep pattern suited to its survival. Small burrowing animals generally sleep by day, because of their exposure to predators in the daylight. Large grazing animals tend to sleep for short periods throughout the twenty-four hour cycle, reflecting their constant need for alertness. Animals with a high metabolism and little fat reserve tend to sleep for longer as a means of conserving energy. For the human being, sleep is a response to the increased dangers posed by darkness and the need to conserve energy. Modern technology may have changed the conditions of our environment but a deeply rooted instinct remains for daylight activity and night-time sleep.

The second function of sleep is as a means of recovery from fatigue. All living organisms have an activity-rest cycle, the two elements existing in relation to each other. Sleep restores optimal functioning, while activity creates the tiredness which promotes sleep. The deprivation of sleep affects mental more than physical ability. Inadequate sleep results in a reduced ability to concentrate, irritability and general disorientation. Laboratory research has demonstrated that these factors are especially pronounced in those deprived of REM or dream sleep. While the body can repair itself adequately during relaxed wakefulness, dreams are essential for mental health. It might even be argued that we sleep in order to dream.

Science tends to confine the reasons for dreaming to the neurobiological. According to J. Allan Hobson's *Activation-Synthesis* hypothesis, dreams are the result of brain chemistry.[3] REM sleep

3. J. Allan Hobson, *The Dreaming Brain. How the Dream Creates both the Sense and Nonsense of Dreams*, (New York: Basic Books, 1988).

is activated by random signals generated in a part of the brain stem known as the pons. This primitive element of the brain does not support higher order mental activities. The forebrain, or limbic brain, then synthesises the output of the pons into as coherent a narrative as possible. In this way the mind creates meaning where it does not actually exist. Inconsistencies in the dream narrative demonstrate how difficult it is for the limbic brain to manage the chaotic output of the pons. The mind may introduce elements that possess a magical or mystical atmosphere in an effort to resolve discrepancies. For Hobson, while a dream may feel religious, it is in effect an entirely biological process. According to this theory dreams are essentially meaningless and perform no higher function than cleansing the brain of misplaced neural stimuli. The function of dreams is confined to sleep itself and the interpretation of dreams is an effort to create sense where there is only nonsense.

Another scientific theory suggests that the key function of dreams is as a regulator of body temperature. REM sleep heats up the brain, while non-REM cools it down. The fact that warm blooded animals have REM during sleep, whereas cold-blooded animals probably do not, strengthens this hypothesis. The alternating cycles between dream and non-dream sleep are driven by the need to keep a steady temperature. Dreams are thereby regarded as a by-product of a *thermoregulation* process.

The research of Mark Solms at the University of Cape Town restores to dreaming a level of intelligence and functionality denied by many neurobiologists.[4] Using functional Magnetic Resonance Imaging (fMRI) technology and Positron Emission Tomography (PET) to map the sleeping brain, he has found a number of mechanisms that make dreams. In sleep, areas of the brain that generate imagery are active even though the eyes are not transmitting signals. Emotional centres of the brain are also active, while those parts involved in rational judgement are relatively dormant. This concurs with Freud's view that emotional drives are given imaginative form in dreams and the function of dreams is to provide a safe outlet for these impulses. Solms has also found some aspects of memory to be less active during

4. M. Solms, *The Neuropsychology of Dreams. A Clinico-Anatomical Study*, (Mahwah, NJ: Lawrence Erlbaum, 1997).

sleep. This means that the mind quickly forgets its own dream imagery, enabling rapid shifts in time and space. Brain mapping technology also points to greater activity in the anterior cingulate cortex during REM sleep. This is the part of the brain concerned with problem solving. Our experience confirms that to 'sleep on' a dilemma is often a useful means of finding a solution.

At a sleep laboratory in the University of California, William Domhoff has catalogued seventeen thousand dreams.[5] Based on the content analysis methods of Calvin Hall, his research has shown that dreams typically differ by age and gender. Children's dreams are fantastic, while adults dream more about the reality of their lives. Men tend to have violent dreams and women's dreams are focused on relationships. Domhoff suggests that dreams are our means of processing reality. The function of dreams is to find our place in the world and integrate new perceptions into the existing sense of personal identity. This point is supported by the fact that young people dream with much greater frequency than the elderly. In our youth the need to make sense of reality is a priority, whereas older people are less likely to be surprised by new experiences.

Science tends to confine the function of dreams to the sleeping state itself: dreams result from the activity of the sleeping brain. Jungian psychology, as we will see in Week Two, takes a different starting point by stating that the dream is inherently meaningful and merits analysis. For Carl Jung dreams serve three purposes: Complementary dreams give an accurate representation of the personality to the person. Compensatory dreams correct imbalances in the individual's conscious attitude. Prospective dreams provide guidance for the future.

Jung regarded dreaming as a 'third state' that combines characteristics of both waking and sleeping. The waking aspect of dreaming is evident in that dreams imagine a person's conscious life. Moreover every dream has a waking dimension in being remembered and retold. A person could not be aware of dreaming or having dreamt if it were an entirely unconscious process. On the other hand, dreams are unconscious since they

---

5. The data is available online at www.dreambank.net and www.dreamresearch.net [accessed 6 November 2007].

lie beyond our sphere of control. They include fantastic situations and impossible switches between time and space. For Jung the nature of dreams is their ability to visualise unconscious processes with conscious imagery. They draw back the veil covering hidden and forgotten aspects of the mind.

Jung recognised that dreams have an automatic ability to discharge anxiety and are beneficial even in the absence of analysis. In cases where a person cannot remember his or her dreams, something 'of the dream-mood will persist after sleep and will linger on into the morning of the day ... Perhaps the drab reality will be touched by the bright golden after-glow of the dream feeling.'[6] The dreaming state relieves stress and somehow helps us to be reconciled with our conflicted lives. However, for Jung, the benefit of unremembered or un-interpreted dreams is relatively weak and transitory. Analysis is the most consistent way of realising the dream's potential.

6. C. G. Jung, 'The Significance of the Unconscious in Individual Education' (1928) CW 17, par. 268.

Day 5: Retrieving the Dream

Sleep science has debunked the idea that dreaming is a rare event. Dream sleep coincides with REM which occurs about five times each night and typically totals ninety minutes. The final dream of the night is most likely to be recalled as it is the longest and we often wake up at its conclusion. However, dreams are generally not easily remembered. In the absence of a conscious effort to recall them, the average person recollects about two dreams each month.

Being a form of immediate experience, the dream tends to be quickly forgotten, withering like a new flower in the morning sun (Ps 90:5-6). Jung attributed difficulty in dream recall to the inattention generally given to the interior life in our culture. All imaginative experiences, such as dreams, tend to be denigrated in a rationally minded society.

The failure to recall dreams also indicates an unwillingness to face the truth about ourselves. Dreams frequently express events that disturb and frighten. The majority of dreams are not sweet. Our resistance to unpleasant thoughts is frequently represented in the dream itself by images of running away from something or someone. A fear of the unknown, the unconscious, compounds the tendency to forget all but the most insistent of dreams.

The principal motive for working with dreams is a desire for improved self-knowledge and sense of direction. However, all personal development, like physical growth, is painful. We both want self-improvement, yet resist the disciplines that will bring it about. An unnecessary busy-ness, endless entertainment, an all-consuming relationship or a lulling routine, serve to distract from personal reflection. Confronting the truth about oneself may involve terminating a favourite destructive-yet-comforting behaviour. Though that truth may be quite obvious to begin, it is often bitter and not easily embraced.

Psychology views resistance as a positive factor in personal development. By identifying an unwillingness to spend time in self-reflection, a person has already taken the first step in overcoming that dynamic. Awareness, coupled with a desire for change is the key to a reduction in resistance to a more considered life. An undertaking to remember and understand your dreams can be an important factor in discovering your true identity. Sharing your dreams with others marks a still deeper commitment to be accountable about yourself.

Making a decision to record your dreams is the most important step in their retrieval. Jung would tell a person who reported an inability to remember dreams: 'You will tonight.'[7] The person who thinks that his or her dreams are important is more likely to remember them. As an expression of this conscious decision, a notebook or voice recorder should be at the bedside to chronicle a few key details of the dream on awakening. These objects act as physical cues that reinforce the desire for dream recall. Dreams tend to be quickly forgotten because of a distraction at the moment of awakening, such as the radio or pressing thoughts about the coming day. If, instead, the note pad or voice recorder is the first item to be noticed, attention will immediately be focused on the task of dream recall.

Spiritual preparation also helps dream retrieval. *Compline*, the night prayer of the church, is a short service of prayer that immediately precedes bedtime. It begins with a recollection of the day's events, being grateful for God's goodness and invoking divine mercy for failings. There follows a psalm, a brief scripture reading and the Canticle of Simeon (Lk 2:29-32). The concluding prayer is an act of trust in God's protection for the night ahead. This shortest of the church's official daily prayer services follows a seven day cycle. It is published as a separate booklet as well being included in full editions of the Breviary.

Night Prayer marks a commitment of your life to God. This

7. C. G. Jung, *Dream Symbols of the Individuation Process: 1. Notes from Seminar held at Bailey Island, Maine, September 20-25, 1936.* Edited by K. Mann, M. E. Harding and E. Bertine. (New York: Kristine Mann Library), 140.

surrender facilitates the passivity required for the onset of sleep. It makes for a more receptive state of mind. An awareness is created that in sleep we can be open to God's presence: 'I slept, but my heart was awake' (Song 5:2). The character of the prayer before bed-time can also be informed by the need to make qualitative distinctions between dreams. In Christian tradition we pray for preservation from evil spirits in sleep and invoke the presence of guardian angels. The desire for a religiously meaningful dream might also be included in prayer. A sample vocal prayer is given in Appendix B.

Dream retrieval is aided by an ability, on awakening, to quickly formulate the key elements of the dream and then transfer these to memory. It is best to awaken without an alarm-clock. The conclusion of a dream often arouses the sleeper of its own accord, whereas disturbing the natural course of sleep could interrupt the narrative. On awakening during the night or at the end of the night's sleep, continue to lie still and consolidate some images from the dream just interrupted or completed. Then reach for your bedside pen or voice recorder button and record some of the key details. Perhaps the best system is a voice activated recorder, whereby some details from the dream can simply be called out as you remain in bed with eyes still closed. Such a device will also capture other sounds from the night such as snoring or somniloquy!

Your initial vocal or written notes, garbled or illegible as they might be, are a surprisingly efficient means of putting together the full dream narrative. Without them, even an impressive dream is likely to be forgotten. At a later point during the same day your memo should be used to write out the full story of the dream. This is best done in the morning when the emotional vitality of the dream is still present.

Prayer can also have a role at the conclusion of dream retrieval. In Hebrew scripture, the receipt of a divinely inspired dream led to a prayer of thanksgiving to God (Gen 28:18-22; Judg 7:15). With the inclusion of such an intention at *Lauds* (morning prayer), the value of some dreams as gifts from God may be better appreciated and their content received with greater respect. A sample morning prayer which explicitly refers to dreams is given in Appendix B.

Consider the practice of telling your dreams to another person over breakfast. This will reinforce the decision to remember your dreams. Being part of a dream-group will likewise promote recall. The habit of keeping a dream journal is another aid to retrieving the dream. After some time you may begin to dream about these ways of sharing your interior life.

Day 6: The Dream Narrative

The first aim of dreamwork is to obtain a clear narrative. Using the details recorded on awakening, write out the story of the dream later that day, preferably in a dedicated journal. The narrative should be thoroughly described as a minor detail may prove crucial to understanding the dream. Some analysts recommend that the dream be retold in the present tense in an effort to retain its sense of present reality. Interpretative comment is withheld for the subsequent dreamwork.

The practice of keeping a journal is of immense value for personal development. Whereas a diary merely catalogues objective events, the journal focuses on interior perceptions. Thoughts and feelings demand self-expression and a personal journal is a safe place to tell the real story of your life. The sense of self-knowledge and acceptance which it promotes is foundational for authentic relationships with others and God. Unawareness, Jung often said, is the greatest sin.[8] When we make conscious our unconscious foibles and weaknesses, we cease to be governed by them. We also discover hidden strengths.

The inclusion of dreams reinforces the aims of the personal journal. Dreaming, like journaling, is a reaction to perceptions. Both activities not only represent life, but also reflect on its underlying meaning. However, dreaming emphasises the unconscious. Conscious experience and norms must be the standard for making judgements. This is a good reason for complementing the dream-log with material from waking experience. Running as a parallel track to our dreams, we can chronicle current events, write about past experiences, pray and record resol-

---

8. 'Ubewusstheit is die grösste Sünde.' H. F. Ellenberger, *The Discovery of the Unconscious. The History and Evolution of Dynamic Psychiatry*, (New York: Basic Books, 1970), 723.

utions. This will provide a conscious corrective to the insights from the unconscious provided by dreams. Without some objective wisdom from our cultural traditions, journaling becomes excessively introspective and narcissistic.

Jung described the dream as a drama played on the stage of the interior life, the *theatrum psychicum* (psychic theater). Its *dramatis personae* (cast) are normally projections of ourselves: 'the dreamer is himself the scene, the player, the prompter, the producer, the author, the public and the critic.'[9] Most dream images represent aspects of the dreamer's own personality that are projected onto the screen of awareness. When a dream portrays another person, it probably represents an aspect of the dreamer rather than the actual person. The image points to its real life counterpart only when it is closely related to the dreamer in waking life. Thus the death of an acquaintance in a dream might mean the loss of that part of your personality which the person represents. Dreams of an employer or authority figure might represent the rule of law and order in your life. The death of close relative or close friend, on the other hand, might refer to your fears for the well-being of that actual person.

Jung noticed that the dream narrative generally follows the same fourfold structure that was used in ancient Greek drama: a beginning (*exposition*), development (*peripeteia*), impasse (*crisis*) and final denouement (*lysis*).[10] This framework might well be kept in mind when writing out the account of your dream:

1. The opening scene is an exposition of the setting and protagonists in the dream. Expressed in theatrical terms, the set is unveiled and the cast are introduced. In the context of dreamwork, the dreamer can state the location and principal concern of the dream at this point.

2. The second phase of the dream narrative is the development of the plot. This is the *peripeteia* or 'strolling around' of the theme. An interaction occurs between the dream actors and their situation. While the initial phase is a fixed scene or

9. C. G. Jung, 'General Aspects of Dream Psychology' (1916/1948) CW 8, par. 509.
10. C. G. Jung, 'On the Nature of Dreams' (1945/1948) CW 8, pars. 561-565; E. C. Whitmont and S. B. Perera, *Dreams. A Portal to the Source*, (London: Routledge, 1989), 69.

tableau, movement now occurs as the story unfolds. The Greek term is reminiscent of the academic conversations held by the philosophers as they walked the precincts of the Athenian Academy with their students. Life itself is a learning journey and movement in dreams can represent its status. Flying upwards or running away in dreams can represent either liberation or an escapist attitude. Falling downward or into something alludes to the return to fundamentals or entrapment. In the Jungian approach, a circular movement (circumambulation) is a statement that life is cyclical, the truth being a still point at the centre of our existence. A leftwards (literally, 'sinister') movement indicates a turning toward the unconscious, while a rightward (literally, 'dexterous') direction points toward the dominance of public concerns and beliefs.

3. The dream narrative then reaches a critical impasse or *crisis*. At this stage something decisive happens. The tension built up through the narrative reaches a culmination. The Greek word 'crisis' suggests 'decisive moment.' A crisis can as much be an opportunity for new life as the destruction of something old. The dreamer's response to the emerging situation is typically one of fear or courage.

4. The fourth phase of a typical dream story is its resolution or *lysis*. The outcome can be a solution which resolves the problem posed by the dream or, in the case of a nightmare, some catastrophe that fulfils the dreamer's fears. The closing image of the dream is usually delivered as a memorable punch line and can possess sufficient energy to awaken the dreamer. The central message of a dream is often to be found in this moment. The absence of a *lysis* indicates that the subject matter of the dream cannot be resolved and hangs in suspension much like a question mark.

Here is an example of the above pattern applied to a short dream recorded by Jung: 'In the sea there lies a treasure (*exposition*). To reach it he has to dive through a narrow opening. This is dangerous but down below he will find a companion (*peripiteia*). The dreamer takes the plunge into the dark (*crisis*) and discovers a beautiful garden in the depths, symmetrically laid out, with a fountain in the centre (*lysis*).'[11] The closing image here can be associated with the garden of Yahweh in the Book of Isaiah (Isa 51:3; 58:11; 61:11).

Dreams are typically told as a story. It can be argued that it is this narration that structures the essentially random process of dreaming. However, for Jung, dreams are inherently meaningful. He noted that a dream is most easily interpreted in the context of its series. A single dream can be accidental and arbitrary. Successive dreams are like pieces of the jigsaw which together form a more complete picture. If dreaming was a haphazard process this would not be the case. The incidence of a recurrent dream indicates the person cannot 'move on' from a particular issue in life. Dream recurrence ceases once the unconscious message has been assimilated.

The Christian faith also views single events in relationship with the individual's whole life. Our option for or against God is not determined by once-off incidents. Just as the Bible tells of a people's developing God image over 1100 years, so our personal histories should be taken in the context of the whole story rather than its individual parts.

---

11. C. G. Jung, *Psychology and Alchemy* (1935/1953) CW 12, par. 154. Parentheses added.

Day 7: A Spirituality of Sleep

Ancient writings generally categorised dreams as being caused by the biological condition of the body or personal memories or supernatural spirits. Religious dreams were typically received by the leaders of society and had implications for society at large. The everyday dreams of ordinary people were not usually regarded as significant. Thus Abraham and Jacob dreamt of their nation's destiny as God's chosen people (Gen 15:12-21; Gen 28:10-22). For the Egyptians it was Pharaoh who received foresight through a dream to make provision for future famine during a time of plenty (Gen 41). The Babylonian king Nebuchadnezzar was warned in a dream that his empire would be cut down because of his pride (Dan 4). In historical oneirology, divinely inspired dreams bestowed healing and insight into the future. Joseph experienced God's soothing affirmation at a time of being hated by his brothers (Gen 37:6-10). In the New Testament, Joseph was warned in dreams to flee to Egypt and avoid Judea on his return (Mt 2:19, 22).

The classical Greeks held that divine revelation could happen during sleep in either of two ways. Homer's view was that we are visited by the gods during sleep. Thus a phantom image from the goddess Athene reassured Penelope in a dream that Odysseus would be safe.[12] In Pythagorean thought, by contrast, the soul was said to leave the body during sleep to roam in the *metaxu*, a sphere of existence between heaven and earth. In that twilight zone it would commune with the gods.

In the Judeo-Christian tradition the debate on the spiritual relevance of sleep has been framed by the following question on the creation story from the Book of Genesis: Did Adam and Eve

---

12. Homer, *The Odyssey*, 4. In the Bible this view is represented by Ps 17:3.

sleep in the Garden of Eden? Or did humanity only begin to sleep after the Fall?

Rather surprisingly most comment held that Adam and Eve only slept after they had sinned. Sleep is the consequence of bodily fatigue and the need to 'suffer for your food' (Gen 3:17), something which was not necessary in Eden. St Paul wrote that both sin and death came into the world as a result of the original fall from grace (Rom 5:12). Tradition has associated both of these realities with sleep.

The passivity of sleep was regarded as making a person more disposed to temptation by demons and so to sin. So plagued by sexual cravings during sleep was the Desert Father, Abba Elias, that one night he had a dream in which three angels appeared.[13] One angel held his hand, one his feet and the third castrated him. Following this dream surgery his sexual obsessions ceased! The monastic tradition developed a timetable which limited sleep so as to protect the monk from temptation at night. As the seventh century Rule of Columbanus said: 'Let the monk come weary to bed and sleep walking, and let him be forced to rise while his sleep is still not finished.'[14]

Elements of Western tradition also link sleep and death. In Greek mythology the god of sleep (Hypnos) and the god of death (Thanatos) were twin brothers. Sleep was generally seen as an anticipation of death, whereby the body is laid low and the mind relinquishes control of itself. Thus God, being eternal, 'will neither slumber nor sleep'(Ps 121:4). St Paul also refers to death as a form of sleep (1 Cor 15:20-51; 1 Thess 4:14).

A more positive understanding of sleep is also evident in tradition. Following the Greek philosopher Socrates (469-399), the Roman poet Cicero (106-43) held that sleep is actually a paradigm for life after death.[15] The sleeping body, apparently lifeless, enjoys life in the *metaxu*. Likewise, physical death masks the new life of the soul freed of temporal and spatial constraints.

The more positive understanding is also evident in the New Testament. The gospels testify to the link between sleep and

13. Palladius, *Lausaic History*, 29.3-4.
14.Columbanus, 'Rules' in G. S. M. Walker (ed), *Sancti Columbani Opera* (Dublin: Institute for Advanced Studies, 1957), 140-141.
15. Cicero, *On Divination*, 1.30.26.

new life in the miracles concerning the resuscitation of Jairus' daughter and Lazarus. While they seemed dead, Jesus reassured the mourners that they were really only asleep (Mk 5:39; Jn 11:14).

Tertullian, one of the earliest Christian theologians, argued that Adam did enjoy sleep in paradise.[16] Sleeping and dreaming is a natural state and part of God's original blessing of creation. It presented Adam with a means of delighting in God's kingdom that waking life could not afford. Tertullian conceived four categories of spiritual dreams:

1. Dreams inspired by demons, who tempt the sleeper with lies and present illusions of divinity. For Tertullian, the majority of spiritual dreams belong to this category.
2. Dreams from God.
3. Dreams based on the imaginative ability of the soul as it 'contemplates the coherence of things.'
4. Dreams of the soul in its 'ecstasy,' a concept peculiar to Tertullian.

This categorisation combines elements of the Homeric and Pythagorean traditions. While the first and second type are based on spiritual influence during sleep, the third and fourth refer to the soul's own ability to commune with the supernatural. Tertullian adhered to the Montanist sect, which expected an imminent *parousia*, or second coming of Christ. The messianic age prophesied in the Old Testament had already come to pass in Christ (Joel 3:1-5; Acts 2:17-21). He felt that Christians now had an immediate sense of God's presence and action in the world and this was especially available through sleep.

A great theologian of the twentieth century, Karl Rahner (1904-1984) adopted Tertullian's position. In Eden, Adam was able to savour God's presence when asleep in a way that was not possible while awake. Adam experienced the benefits of dreaming in an automatic way. Humanity, in its fallen state, must analyse the dream in order to find traces of God's presence. In short, the ability to sleep is a sign of God's love, a time when we can be paradoxically awake to God's presence:

---

16. Tertullian, *De Anima*, 47.

Is it not the case that the brightness of the day's consciousness is delightful only because a gentle twilight can always carry it over softly into the gentle, tired stillness of sleep! Don't we renounce in sleep the clear sharpness of the light of day, the privilege of being autonomous persons who are thereby imprisoned in the confines of the consciously given, in order to yield ourselves quietly again to a life which is not ours but which in compensation is wise and limitless, because it moves and acts in yon dark kingdom where every individual is ever caught up in the movement of the All?

Rahner's comments connect the spirituality of sleep to a detachment from daily preoccupations. On falling asleep we cede control of both body and soul. This yielding of consciousness is a prerequisite of sleep and is evocative of the resignation into God's hands which precedes a peaceful death. A reluctance to fall asleep may well be associated with the ultimate relinquishing of self-control in death. It takes an attitude of trust to fall asleep. Supporting that trust there is the faith, whether conscious or unconscious, that we are being cared for by a higher power.

17. K. Rahner, 'A Spiritual Dialogue at Evening: on Sleep, Prayer and Other Subjects,' *Theological Investigations* 3 (London: DLT, 1967), 223.

WEEK TWO

Psychology

Listen to this dream. Gen 37:6

Day 8:
S. Freud, The Interpretation of Dreams (1900)

The psychology of Sigmund Freud (1856-1939) revolutionised our understanding of human nature. Whereas classical philosophy defined the human being as 'an individual substance of a rational nature' (Boethius), Freud appreciated the influence of non-rational factors over which we have little control. These are evident in slips of the tongue ('Freudian slips') that are not as accidental as they appear. For Freud, the instincts and repressed memories that constitute the unconscious motivate behaviour as much as conscious faculties. While these forces can influence daytime life, they are especially active in dreams when repressed material becomes part of mental activity.

Freud conceived the unconscious as a morass of desires that are both personally and socially unacceptable. These instinctual wishes, which he called the *id*, are predominantly sexual in nature (that is, *libidinal*) and begin in early childhood. The person's socially conditioned moral standpoint, the *censor* or *superego*, denies the free gratification of the instinctual drive. The conflict between the impulsive id and the controlling censor is resolved by the centre of consciousness, the *ego*. During sleep the managing efforts of the ego are compromised by a weakening of the censor. Dreams express and represent unconscious desires and ambitions.

In *The Interpretation of Dreams*, Freud argued that the operation of the censor is modified rather than lost during sleep. Dreams strive to balance the need for rest with the expression of deep seated instincts. In other words, dreaming acts in a parallel way to the repressive activity of consciousness. While dreams are instigated by stimulating unconscious wishes and relieve the tension caused by those wishes, they also preserve sleep: 'Dreams are the guardians of sleep and not its disturbers.'[1] When a sleeper

---

1.S. Freud, *The Interpretation of Dreams*. J. Strachey (ed). *The Standard*

is awoken, the dream has not adequately discharged its sleep-preserving function. The activity of the censor ensures that even remembered dreams are normally soon forgotten.

Freud used the term 'Traumarbeit' (*dreamwork*) to describe the means by which dreams combine their unconscious revealing and sleep-preserving function. It chiefly occurs in the relationship between the *manifest* and *latent* aspects of a dream. The manifest dream is the dream as it appears. The latent dream is the underlying subject matter that is denied full expression. Freud held that manifest images are a distortion of the latent message of the dream. While in some dreams, an obvious association exists between the manifest and latent content, normally the latent facts are not immediately recognisable. For Freud, the true meaning of the dream is not easily deciphered.

In continuity with nineteenth century oneirology, Freud explained many dreams as the result of bodily or environmental factors. A person who has eaten salty food might be awoken by thirst or appease that desire by dreams of drinking. In the former case the wish overpowers the need to sleep, whereas in the latter the dream succeeds in preserving sleep. Such *dreams of convenience* imagine a want being satisfied in order to distract the dreamer from a stimulating wish and so allow sleep to continue. The latent content of a dream is frequently manifested in terms of the previous day's events, the *day residue*.

Freud considered the influence of conscious factors in dreams to be relatively minor in comparison with unconscious sources. The day residue is simply a vehicle for the representation of repressed mental content. It is in this point that Freud's theory was most original. While the majority of dreams deal with superficial everyday matters, they actually arise from a desire for the fulfillment of deep-seated sexual wishes that have been repressed since infancy. Dreams are 'a revival of ... childhood, of the instinctual impulses which dominated it and of the methods of expression which were then available.'[2] Horrible childhood fantasies such as killing one parent and marrying the other (the *Oedipus* or *Electra* complex) which would not be enter-

Edition of the Complete Psychological Works of Sigmund Freud, IV-V, (London: Hogarth Press, 1953), 233.
2. S. Freud, *The Interpretation of Dreams,* 548.

tained during waking life are more readily asserted at night. However, this happens in a disguised way that attempts not to disturb the sleeper from the primary physical need for rest.

The Interpretation of Dreams describes four mechanisms by which the dreamwork is achieved. *Condensation* refers to the connection of two or more images, normally separate in daily life, into one dream image. This makes the underlying content more complex than the manifest image. *Displacement* converts the latent content of a dream into a related but less disturbing subject matter. Thus a situation of great importance, such as the death of a parent, might be imagined by the destruction of something of less significance which also represents a source of life and protection. *Plastic representation* or *concretising* refers to the presentation of abstract issues in a personified or narrative form. Finally, the unconscious processes of making the dream into a coherent narrative and all subsequent conscious analysis is a *secondary revision* or *secondary elaboration*. This risks a further distortion of the dream's original content.

In Freudian oneirology, the analysis of dreams rather than the dream itself is the *via regia* (the royal road) to understanding the unconscious mind. The manifest dream is a distortion of the unconscious image that can only be overcome through professional dream analysis. The psychoanalyst uncovers the hidden content behind the dream imagery: 'Well then, the patient has told us a dream which we are to interpret. ... We decide to concern ourselves as little as possible with what we have heard, with the *manifest* dream.'[3] In other words, dream analysis is a reversal of the dreamwork.

Freud conducted his analytical sessions with the patient relaxed on a couch and out of the direct view of the analyst. The client would narrate a dream and be invited to *free associate* with the different parts of the dream as honestly as possible. The analyst adopted an impartial attitude so as to facilitate the client's willingness to overcome repressing the unconscious. Freud referred every image in the dream backward to some unfulfilled wish from childhood. He would typically make associ-

3. S. Freud, 'New Introductory Lectures on Psychoanalysis', J. Strachey (ed), *The Standard Edition of the Complete Psychological Works of Sigmund Freud*, XXII. (London: Hogarth Press, 1964), 10.

ations with sexual issues. Elongated dream objects were seen as representing the penis, while female genitalia were imaged by hollow items. The freedom of association in dream analysis was thereby restricted to sexual connotations. This would prove a point of contention with Jung who broadened the rationale of dream images in his psychology.

The opening chapter of *The Interpretation of Dreams* is a history of oneirology. While Freud appreciated the respect for dreams in ancient societies, he was critical of their approach. In particular he rejected as pre-modern any belief in a supernatural dream source. Freud understood faith in God as an illusion based on the desire for an adequate parent. He explained spiritual dreams by the fact that unconscious forces can be so repressed as to seem alien and thereby given a godly status. Freudian analysis is thoroughly atheistic. The couch replaces the dream sanctuary as the setting for dreamwork and the unconscious rather than God was regarded as the source for the healing power of dreams.

C. G. Jung at Bailey Island, New York in 1936

Day 9:
C. G. Jung, Memories, Dreams, Reflections (1963)

Carl Gustav Jung was born on 26 July 1875 in Kesswill, Switzerland. His forebears were mainly doctors and pastors, something which may explain his lifelong concern for healing and religion. As a child it confused Jung that Jesus was presented as both sweet and threatening. His father, a Lutheran pastor, preached sermons that were boring and death oriented. By contrast, dreams offered him vital experiences of the divine that were by turn fascinating and terrifying.[4]

In one childhood dream, when he was three or four years of age, Jung found himself in a richly brocaded underground chamber. On a throne at the end of the room was a large phallic-shaped object, surrounded by a bright aura. The image possessed the awe-inspiring characteristics of the Almighty. The adult Jung interpreted it as pointing out the location of divine presence: buried in the depths of the psyche and awaiting discovery through the experience of the unconscious.

A defining moment in Jung's spiritual journey was reached when, aged twelve, he had a pre-Confirmation discussion with his father on the doctrine of the Trinity. Jung was disappointed by his father's blind submission to the dogma. Soon afterwards on a visit to the cathedral in Basel, Jung willed himself to believe that it was God's house. Three nights later he had a dream in which God was seated in majesty. A turd dropped out of the throne and shattered the resplendent roof of the cathedral. Jung interpreted the dream as God's displeasure with institutionalised Christianity. From this time on, Jung resisted conventional religion, while remaining fascinated by the experience of God within.

4. C. G. Jung, *Memories, Dreams, Reflections*, Edited by A. Jaffé and translated by R. and C. Winston (New York: Random House, 1963), 11-40.

As a newly qualified psychiatric doctor, Jung began to pay attention to his patients' dreams after reading *The Interpretation of Dreams* in 1901. He subsequently became a devoted disciple of Freud. However the collaboration would end by 1913 mainly because Freud tended to interpret dream images as a substitution for the sex drive. Jung, on the other hand, understood even sexual images in dreams as symbolic of other issues. Freud conceived the ego as the centre of the personality. Jung, by contrast, conceived the indwelling God-image, the *Self*, to be at the centre.

Following the break with Freud, Jung embarked on an intensive process of personal reflection that focused on his dreams. In *Psychological Types* (1921) he formulated the key points of his psychology. He conceived the most fundamental division in the personality (the *psyche*) between the *conscious* and the *unconscious*. Consciousness is ordinary awareness that occurs when a person realises 'I am'. In the conscious, the *personal conscious* is one's own experience, whereas the *collective conscious* represents social-cultural influences.

The unconscious is made up of perceptions which have been forgotten, or never consciously noted. As well as personal contents it possesses the *archetypes*, inherited tendencies toward ideas or patterns of behaviour seen in all humanity. They are expressed in some dreams and are projected in cultural motifs, fairy-tales and myths. Jung stressed that the archetypes are not particular images but rather the idea behind them. To express the childhood instinct that the world is a dangerous place, my prehistoric ancestors might have dreamt of being chased by a crocodile. My own childhood expression of this idea was the recurring dream of being chased by a Volkswagen Beetle, its open bonnet snapping at my heels.

Jung held that consciousness of the archetypes is essential to mental health and explained the imbalances of Western society by a loss of such contact. He argued that popular images of God and religious dogmas are projected archetypes. In the absence of a public communication of belief this explains the common ground between religions. In other words, we are born with a naturally occurring predisposition towards the spiritual that is relatively independent of social influence. The most central archetype, the Self, is akin to belief in the indwelling of God.

The personal dimension of the unconscious contains the *complexes*, personal 'issues' which emotionally engage with the conscious, causing involuntary blockages in speech and memory. A person who has a childhood car accident may develop a complex around road safety, while everyone else can address the problem in a calm manner. The autonomous nature of the complex makes it capable of being personified in dreams. As Jungians say, a particular complex can be *constellated* by a dream image. While a complex is typically perceived as negative it can play a positive role in maturation by pointing out semi-conscious memories that request attention.

At the core of many personal complexes lies an archetype. For example, an uneasy relationship between male siblings might create abnormal feelings around the term 'brother'. This personal situation also has archetypal dimensions. Rivalry between two brothers for their parents' blessing is a scenario that has been played out since the dawn of humanity. Biblical incidents of the 'hostile brothers' archetype include Cain and Abel (Gen 4), Esau and Jacob (Gen 25-27) and the Elder and Prodigal sons (Lk 15:11-32). An understanding of these stories can locate each new experience of the complex within its archetypal context and help relativise its intensity.

Jung characterised the rapport between the conscious and unconscious as an *Auseinandersetzung* or confrontational dialogue. *Individuation* (maturity) is forged in the intra-personal tension between the two parts of the psyche. The conscious protects the personality from possession by the chaotic unconscious. A dominant unconscious reduces the strength of the conscious to that of its role in dreams. On the other hand, a repressed unconscious makes for a superficial life.

Jung's reputation grew throughout the 1930s and 1940s and he gained worldwide recognition during his lifetime. He maintained a large private psychotherapeutic practice and conducted seminars, including those on dreams at Swanage (England) in 1925, Bailey Island (New York) in 1936 and Zürich from 1928-1930. He would analyse, on average, two thousand dreams each year. Jung wrote books on the Trinity, Christ and the problem of evil, which drew on esoteric as well as orthodox ideas. In these works he controversially argued that the Christian image of God was excessively sanitised and should include the element of darkness. When he was asked in a BBC interview: 'Do you believe in God?' He replied: 'I *know*. I don't need to believe. I know.'[5] For Jung, God was primarily an experience and only secondarily an absolute being. While he did not adhere to organised religion, he possessed a strong intuitive faith, using the Bible and other Christian sources in a way that was unique among psychologists.

Ever since he was a child, Jung aimed to reform Christianity so that it would connect with the vitality of religious experience. Church based worship should be replaced by direct knowledge of God. He claimed that although creeds and dogmas are useful guides to religious truths, they are in themselves lifeless. Dreams, on the other hand, as an immediate form of experience, can suitably convey the dynamism of religion. Shortly before his death in 1961, Jung dreamt of a 'big, round block of stone in a high bare place.'[6] The image gave him a sense of fulfilment. What had been buried in a childhood dream was now revealed. Jung had accomplished the definition of maturity set out in his autobiography: 'the self-realisation of the unconscious.'[7]

5. W. McGuire and R. F. C. Hull (eds), C. G. *Jung Speaking. Interviews and Encounters*, (Princeton, NJ: Princeton University Press, 1977), 428.
6. B. Hannah, *Jung: His Life and Work* (New York: G. P. Putnam's Sons, 1976), 347.
7. C. G. Jung, *Memories, Dreams, Reflections*, 3.

Day 10: Types of Dreams

Not all dreams are of equal importance. In a little known seminar on children's dreams Jung qualitatively ranked four types:[8]

1. Dreams that are a reaction to the situation of the dreamer.
These dreams typically incorporate disturbances from the sleeper's physical environment or replay the events of the previous day. Factors like a passing noise, a smell or a change in bedroom temperature can be fitted into the imagery of the dream. Stimuli from the sleeper's environment tend to be represented in dreams as they occur and in a way that preserves sleep. Other dreams of this type are a response to the condition of the sleeping body. Feeling thirsty you may dream of drinking water, thereby satisfying a need while preserving sleep. An uncomfortable sleeping position might prompt a dream that leads to a change of posture.

2. Dreams which represent an unconscious response to consciously remembered events.
Jung's second type is based on the operation of the unconscious. It shows the ability of the mind, not just to remember, but to reflect on the meaning of everyday experience. Not all perceptions are consciously noted. Negative or challenging events are especially prone to slipping into the unconscious. This type of dream helps process unconscious perception.

It was with regard to these dreams that Jung referred to a complementary function. Dreams represent our waking life concerns. According to a Latin proverb: 'The dog dreams of bread,

---

8. C. G. Jung, *Psychological Interpretation of Children's Dreams. Notes on Lectures given at the Eidgenössische Technische Hochschule, Zürich: 1938-1939.* (New York: Kristine Mann Library, 1939), 4-5.

the fisherman of fish.'[9] For example: 'When you are hungry you dream of food, and if you are too hot in bed you can dream of snow. ... People who are long in bed on account of fractured bones or other causes often dream of taking exceptionally long walks, or that they are jumping or dancing. Soldiers in the trenches used to dream of peaceful Sundays at home.'[10] Some of these dreams do not simply represent life but shed new light on its underlying meaning. For example a businessman who had partly unwittingly become involved in a fraudulent deal dreamt that 'his hands and forearms were covered with black dirt.'[11] The dream reflected and enlarged the man's semi-awareness of being 'up to his arms' in a messy situation.

3. Dreams that come from the unconscious to alter the conscious attitude.

Jung's psychology attaches much more importance to dreaming than most theories of human behaviour. The Greek philosopher Plato (427-347) believed that dreaming was merely a refuge for the irrational self.[12] Even Freud held that dreams are a form of hysteria, by which the mind conceals disturbing mental contents. Most scientists confine the purpose of dreams to a form of mental hygiene. The Jungian approach proposes these third and the fourth categories because sometimes the unconscious is not merely repetitive or reactive, but also presents valuable new insights for our attention. In dreaming we are not simply responding to neurological stimuli, nor replaying the past, but are sometimes capable of gaining a more intelligent perspective on our situation.

Jung conceived two key categories of dreams in this third type. *Compensatory dreams* help establish or maintain mental balance by challenging consciously held presumptions. This is

9. 'Canis panem somniat, piscator pisces.' C. G. Jung, *Symbols of Transformation* (1912/1952) CW 5, par. 9.
10. C. G. Jung, *Modern Psychology. Notes on Lectures given at the Eidgenössische Technische Hochschule, Zürich from October 1933- July 1935.* (New York: Kristine Mann Library, 1959), Vol. 1, 135.
11. C. G. Jung, 'Flying Saucers: A Modern Myth of Things Seen in the Sky' (1958) CW 10, par. 826.
12. Plato, *The Republic*, 9.571c.

illustrated in the dream recounted to Jung by a retired army general.[13] In it the general was among a group of officers under inspection. The dreamer was taken by surprise when, instead of asking him a technical question, the commander demanded a definition of beauty. He was embarrassed at not being able to reply, especially as the next man, a young officer, gave an excellent answer. In the dream analysis, the general associated the officer with himself as a youth. He remembered his youthful interest in art and how this had been lost through years of military rigidity. The dream thus prompted the dreamer to consider the importance of the hidden artistic dimension in his life.

Prospective dreams provide a prognosis for the personality, in response to its current situation. For example, in the case of a prurient female client, dreams set in unsavoury surrounding were reported.[14] At one point these dreams specified what would happen if she walked alone in the woods. One week later it transpired that the woman was indeed the victim of a sexual assault in a forest. Jung opined that the dream had forewarned the patient of the dangers repressed desires would create in her waking life.

4. Dreams that bear no relation to the conscious situation.
Fourthly, and most profoundly are dreams that come from the collective unconscious. These rare dreams cannot be interpreted using physical or psychological cues from the sleeper's environment. They have no obvious link to the conscious situation. Nor are they simply an unconscious response to the person's lifestyle. Such dreams remind us of the presence of an innate archetypal wisdom in our lives that both reassures and directs according to its own agenda. This kind of dream points toward the presence of God in our lives.

Jung often described the fourth type as the 'big' dream, all others being 'little' dreams. This simpler schema was learnt from the Elgonyi of Uganda with whom Jung visited in 1925. He was puzzled by this people's reticence to share their dreams

---

13. C. G. Jung, 'Analytical Psychology and Education: Three Lectures' (1926/1946) CW 17, par. 187.
14. C. G. Jung, 'Symbols and the Interpretation of Dreams' (1961) CW 18, par. 471.

since they had been so trusting of him in all other matters. A local medicine man explained that while 'little' dreams were inconsequential, great attention had been paid to 'big' dreams as they offered valuable guidance. However, in modern times all dream analysis was regarded as redundant. The 'little' dream did not merit attention and with the advent of British administration 'big' dreams no longer occurred. The District Commissioner now provided all the crucial advice that the people needed! Among the Elgonyi the 'big' dream alone was considered of divine origin and tended to be given to the leaders. Traditionally, a 'big' dream merited a village meeting as it was seen to have social import.

In Jung's description the *little* dream comes from the personal sphere and its meaning concerns the dreamer. Such dreams are quickly forgotten because they reflect immediate concerns. They replay events from the previous day and are caused by the day residue, the physical environment of the sleeper, or the personal unconscious. Even compensatory and prospective dreams are normally 'little' since they answer to the conscious life of the dreamer.

The *big* dream is typically remembered for a lifetime and stands out as a landmark on the life journey. It adds information to consciousness, having contents that cannot be associated with lived memory. While it is coloured by the individual context it seems to come from a different level. The big dream's origin is the archetypes of the collective unconscious and its orientation is towards universal concerns. Such dreams are typically set in an archaic time and are numinous, possessing an awe-inspiring beauty. Big dreams are concerned with crucial issues and their striking quality impels a person to share the experience with others. The 'big' dream is infrequent with a tendency to occur at moments of transition such as childhood, puberty, mid-life and prior to death. The subjective situation is the key to interpreting 'small' dreams. The meaning of 'big' dreams, by contrast, can be uncovered principally by finding similar cultural expressions of the archetypal situation expressed in the dream.

Day 11: The Functions of Dreams

Today's reading will explore the two key functions of dreams, mentioned yesterday.

The Compensation Function

Jung principally described the purpose of dreams as compensatory. As we go through life, ego-centred concerns are dominant and unconscious needs tend to be thrust into the background. Being repressed these accumulate over time and gather strength. The excluded or neglected thoughts are then, in compensation, asserted by the unconscious, normally through dreams.

Compensation is an involuntary or natural function. Jung associated it with homeostasis by which the body maintains a balanced metabolism. To keep a steady temperature the body perspires when it is hot and shivers when cold. In the same way a compensatory relationship between the conscious and unconscious acts to preserve mental balance.

The aspect of dream compensation depends on the situation of the dreamer. Where relations between the conscious and unconscious are harmonious, dreams will tend to be complementary in scope. However, there is normally some disequilibrium between the two spheres of the personality. A dominant conscious is compensated by a more assertive unconscious and *vice versa*. The conscious and unconscious act as irritants to each other. This intra-personal tension is a key source of psychic energy: 'Life is born only of the spark of opposites.'[15]

The early works of Jung understood compensation in the relationship between the personal conscious and the personal unconscious. In such cases the compensation is easily recog-

---

15. C. G. Jung, 'The Psychology of the Unconscious' (1917/1926/1943) CW 7, par. 78.

nised once the needs of the dreamer are understood. For example, the person who is manifestly extraverted will have their latent introversion asserted in dreams of being thoughtfully alone. On the other hand, the publicly shy person will dream of being affable and at ease in company. Jung later went on to recognise an element of compensation from the collective unconscious. The distortions of an individual's equilibrium are caused to some extent by cultural imbalances. In compensation, the unconscious archetypes are asserted through dreams. Jung was critical of the focus on science and material wealth in Western culture. By contrast, dreams emphasise the imaginative and the spiritual and so inherently effect a counter-cultural compensation.

When the conscious personality is in crisis, compensation may well assume a positive tone. In such cases there may be momentous encounters with the rich and famous, thereby redressing a sense of low self-esteem. In the Book of Genesis, Joseph was the butt of ongoing contempt by his eleven older brothers (Gen 37:3-4). He then had two dreams which served to compensate his sense of inferiority (Gen 37:6-7, 9-10). In the first he saw sheaves of corn bow down before him. It imaged the honour bestowed on him by God, who, like corn, is a source of life. When Joseph told the dream to his siblings, their negative reaction provided the context for an even more exaggerated image of divine election in a second dream. In it the sun, moon and eleven stars bowed down before Joseph. This one annoyed his brothers so much that they kidnapped their brother and sold him as a slave into Egypt.

When the conscious personality is self-satisfied, the unconscious will act negatively. For instance, a man who was proud of his moral lifestyle dreamt of a drunken tramp wallowing in a roadside ditch. In this case 'the dream was attempting to deflate his exalted opinion of himself'.[16] Jung cited a dream of the Babylonian King Nebuchadnezzar in the Book of Daniel (Dan 4) as an example of negative compensation.[17] In the dream the king

16. C. G. Jung, 'Symbols and the Interpretation of Dreams' (1961) CW 18, par. 507.
17. C. G. Jung, 'General Aspects of Dreams Psychology' (1916/1948) CW 8, par. 485.

saw an abundant tree growing up to heaven. It supported wildlife and cast a shadow over the earth. Then one came from above to prune back the tree so that only the stump remained. Consistent with Jungian principles of dream interpretation, Daniel understood the dream as a response to the conscious life of the dreamer. He accurately saw it as a prediction of the king's fall from greatness. However, God's judgement, while elicited by Nebuchadnezzar's own pride, was concealed from him by that same vanity. Only Daniel could understand the dream's latent meaning. Interpreted psychologically, the 'holy watcher' which spoke in the dream was simply Nebuchadnezzar's unconscious acting in compensation against his degenerate lifestyle (Dan 4:14-15).

The Prospective Function

We often go to bed wondering what the future will bring. Our dreams process these forward-looking thoughts as much as they do the memory of past events. Jung understood prospective dreams as offering guidance for the future, or a best guess as to what the future might hold. On this point, Jung's oneirology contrasts with Freud's regressive analysis, which approached the dream as an expression of unresolved needs from childhood.

The prospective function features in many biblical dreams. Abram dreamt about the destiny of his family (Gen 15:12-15). Joseph applied a predictive interpretation to Pharaoh's dreams in Genesis 41. The four dreams of the New Testament Joseph all provided direction for the Holy Family (Mt 1-2). The Magi interpreted their dream as a warning to avoid future contact with Herod (Mt 2:12). Some of the 'night visions' in the Acts of the Apostles likewise concern the practical guidance offered by dreams to St Paul on his journeys (Acts 16:9-10; Acts 23:11).

Many of Jung's references to the prospective function relate it to the situation of the dreamer. Dreams may, for example, compensate for a feeling of inadequacy by painting a hopeful vision of the future. Likewise a self-destructive lifestyle may lead to warnings of disaster in dreams. In other places, Jung conceived the prospective function as connected to the archetypal elements of the unconscious. This demonstrates that the unconscious has an autonomous role in setting out life's goals and is not always a reaction to the conscious situation.

Jung's description of the prospective function of dreams is notably similar to our understanding of prophecy in the Bible. The prophets' concern for the future of Israel was based on divinely inspired insight into its current situation rather than a magical foreknowledge. The prophets warned their people of the consequences of corrupt living, or predicted better times in the midst of disaster. Rather than aiming to satisfy human curiosity for foreknowledge, the genuine prophet highlighted the need for prayer and conversion (Jer 28:8-9; 1 Kings 22:8). Likewise, Jung grounded the meaning and purpose of precognitive dreams in the circumstances of the individual.

In a commentary on the 'third secret' of Fatima, Cardinal Ratzinger wrote that predictive visions should be interpreted symbolically, not literally.[18] Divine revelation engages the capacities and respects the limits of the recipient. Visions of the future are based on the contemporary situation. The Fatima visionaries' image of a steep mountain and a city in ruins are read as images for the struggle involved in humanity's progress and the destruction which characterised the twentieth century. In particular, the Fatima messages were based on the trauma of a world ravaged by war in 1917. Ratzinger affirms Jung's basic point: prospective visions do not so much concern knowledge of the time to come, as insight into the future insofar as it is contained in the present.

However, the prospective function is sometimes powerful enough to create an actual precognition. St John Bosco (1815-1888), founder of the Salesian congregation, famously had precognitive dreams. On one occasion, as a child, he dreamt of the Latin text which his teacher would dictate the following day.[19] That night he went to his desk and transcribed the dream revelation. The next day, owing to time constraints, the teacher dictated just half of the passage. To the master's amazement, the pupil also presented those parts of the text which had not been dictated.

Such precognitive dreams are a rare occurrence. A dream's

18. J. Ratzinger, 'Theological Commentary' in Congregation for the Doctrine of the Faith, *The Message of Fatima* (Libreria Editrice Vaticana, 2000), 40-41.
19. P. Meseguer, *The Secret of Dreams* (London: Burns and Oates, 1960), 121.

conjecture is labelled precognitive when it happens to be realised; however, many dream predictions do not come to pass. The fact that we dream of something happening, does not make it happen, but suggests it could. A dream's predictive ability can only be determined with hindsight and is effectively a coincidence of conjecture with reality. In Jung's view, the experience of *déjà vu* has a similar dynamic.[20] He explained it as the fulfillment of a half-remembered precognitive dream in conscious life.

It is normal for the precognition to take place just a little before or even during the incident. Perhaps it is something of the same sensitivity which incorporates images from the sleeper's environment that also enables minute signals of immanent events to be picked up. Such instances can also be understood as a form of telepathy, whereby the dream is an inexplicable communication between an event or person and the sleeper. When people are involved they are likely to be acquaintances. A mother and child are especially capable of parallel and telepathic dreams.

---

20. C. G. Jung, 'On Synchronicity' (1951) CW 8, par. 974.

Day 12: Dream-Speech

Freud held that dreams conceal the unconscious in order to pre-serve sleep from its disturbing contents. For Jung, by contrast, dreams reveal the hidden mind. They use a poetic speech that is often difficult to grasp. This makes the message more bearable and ultimately facilitates self-disclosure. To adopt lines from Emily Dickinson, dreams

> Tell all the Truth but tell it slant –
> Success in Circuit lies
> Too bright for our infirm delight
> The Truth's superb surprise.[21]

Experiencing a personal truth is not simply a matter of factual understanding. The dream elucidates the matter at hand with all of its emotional complexity and eventually presents a far more rounded picture of the issue.

The dream uses a variety of linguistic tools to convey its mes-sage. In the phrase of Heinrich von Schubert (1780-1860) dreams are a 'picture language' (*Traumbildsprache*) that depict the per-sonality through images rather than words. These should not be taken at face value. Most items in a dream are a portrayal of some aspect of the dreamer's own life whether forgotten, exist-ing or potential.

For example, as imagined in a dream, the means of con-veyance represent the ways in which a dreamer is moved or mo-tivated in life. Travelling by public transport implies reliance on collective values. Being a passenger might signify a failure to as-sert one's own identity, a 'not being in the driver's seat' of life. Dreams of flying through the air indicate having lost touch with reality. Cycling, on the other hand, is an image for being both

---

21. E. Dickinson, 'Tell All the Truth' in R. W. Franklin (ed), *The Poems of Emily Dickinson*, (Cambridge, MA: Belknap Press of Harvard University, 1998), poem 1129.

grounded and self-propelled. Struggling through mud may indicate being stuck. Crossing a bridge in a dream can represent a time of transition in your life. Walking over a bridge with someone, might show that person's role as one who 'carries you over' from one stage in life to the next. Dreams of sailing in fine weather are typically mystical, as there is a sense of being supported by something vast and moved by an invisible power.

Imaginative language increases in strength from straightforward representations of memories, to still more complex *similes* and *metaphors*. A dream using the device of a simile might begin with a straightforward memory such as your sympathising with the bereaved at a funeral and then move on to depict castles or fortresses. Here the interpretation might be that the dreamer has been like a tower of strength for the bereaved. It is perhaps more common for the dream images to make comparisons in a metaphorical way ('You are a tower of strength'), in which case the dream might be of castles and have no direct connection with the funeral. Dreams tend to emphasise the meaning of an experience rather than simply replay it from memory.

Dream images may employ the pun whereby a colloquialism or a play on words, is depicted. For example, an opinionated woman could not be persuaded by her analyst to become more tolerant.[22] In a dream she was invited to an important function. She was graciously received at the front door of a mansion and told that her friends were awaiting her arrival. However, she then walked into a cowshed. The woman soon accepted that she was behaving like an 'old cow.'

In another case the central image in a student's dream resembled Jacob's ladder.[23] As he spoke about this image the dreamer emphasised the wooden material which made up the ladder. The analyst interpreted this as pointing to the aspirational or 'would' nature of his spiritual life.

Hyperbole adds emphasis to a point through exaggeration. This is a quintessential figure of dream-speech since dreams

22. C. G. Jung, 'Symbols and the Interpretation of Dreams' (1961) CW 18, par. 463.
23. J. Taylor, 'Traversing the Living Labyrinth' in K. Bulkeley (ed), *Among all these Dreamers. Essays on Dreaming and Modern Society* (Albany, NY: SUNY, 1996), 148-150.

usually intensify expression, especially the emotions. The outrageous proportions of dream images makes the message more forceful. In one case a young man dreamt that his father was behaving in a drunken and disorderly manner while driving a car.[24] This was completely out of character for the father. The son's relationship with his father was actually so perfect that he had failed to develop his own identity. The dream compensated the son's excessively idealistic image.

The *symbol* is the most important type of dream speech. The term comes from the Greek language and means 'thrown together.' In classical Greece, symbols referred to the halves of a coin which two parties to an agreement broke and shared. It was originally, therefore, a visible token of something that also pointed to a missing part.

Jung developed a specific understanding of the term in contrast with that of Freud. According to Freud, dream images refer to prior causes in the dreamer's childhood. This reduced the meaning of dream images to *signs*, that is, indicators of another definite fact or item. Symbols, on the other hand, point to realities that are not fully realised in this world. Both signs and symbols stand for something other than what is actually depicted. However, signs can be readily translated into material realities. Symbols, on the other hand, do not exhaust their meaning in physical reality and are oriented to spiritual realities. Thus the 'symbolic' closely resembles the 'sacramental'. Both words suggest concrete reminders of invisible or supernatural realities.

For Jung a symbol's impact is generally organised by the principle of compensation. If the archetypal dimension is denied consciousness it finds a covert outlet through dream symbols. It produces a symbol which supersedes the impasse between the conscious and the unconscious and reconciles the two fundamental elements of the psyche. Such symbols are, in Jungian terminology, produced by the psyche's *transcendent function* and are perceived as gift, a *tertium non datur* (unforeseen third).

In Jung's own case one such reconciling symbol was provided by a dream set in Liverpool in 1919.[25] He dreamt of walking

---

24. C. G. Jung, 'The Practical Use of Dream Analysis' (1934) CW 16, pars. 335-336.
25. C. G. Jung, *Memories, Dreams, Reflections*, 197-199.

through its streets with a group of friends on a rainy night. The rain cleared as they moved to the city centre. They arrived at the central intersection from which radiated several avenues. In the brightly illuminated central point grew a magnolia tree with red blossoms of outstanding beauty. He had this dream following the personal crisis of his break with Freud. This image gave him a sense of inner peace and purpose at the 'liver' or core of his being.

The dream symbol typically scores an emotional resonance with a person. Ordinary language tends to be bland and superficial. Symbols, on the other hand, have the capacity to integrate the rational and the emotional, the physical and the spiritual. In particular, symbols evoke that sense of the numinous that is traditionally associated with a religious event.

Dream symbols have the same potential as religious symbols for transfiguring a person's existence with possibilities that cannot be logically foreseen. Jung claimed that in our time the symbols found in religious traditions have become stale and boring. They have effectively been reduced to signs of some other material reality. On the other hand, archetypal or 'big' dreams continue to provide dynamic reminders of the spiritual realm. In the pursuit of religious experience, Jung advocated a return to the symbolising language of the dream.

Day 13: The Dramatis Personae of Dreams

Apart from those closely related to us, the characters that perform on our dream stage at night represent aspects of our own personality. Jung described a sizeable number of stock actors and proposed that a progressive relationship exists between them in the process of reaching maturity. Today we look at some of the most important figures, in their order of appearance.

The centre of personal consciousness or self-awareness is the *ego*. In psychology the term does not imply 'egotism' but is simply the awareness of being 'me'. The ego usually participates directly in the action of the dream. The dream ego is typically weaker and more timid than its counterpart in waking life. It better reflects the reality of our vulnerability. In some dreams the ego is a passive observer, an onlooker in the drama of life.

The *persona* is the aspect of the person on display to the outer world. It represents the energy invested in social roles. The term is derived from the Greek word for 'mask' and recalls the facial devices used by actors in classical Greek drama.

Some investment in standardised roles is necessary for successful interaction. A doctor, a shopkeeper or a teacher can best fulfil their role when they dress and behave in the ways expected of them. However the persona becomes problematic when it is equated with the ego. We are much more than our social roles. A respect for the unconscious makes possible a separation between the ego and the persona. Once this occurs the psychic energy needed to maintain the persona is made available to the psyche as a whole. The persona is typically represented in dreams by an emphasis on clothing or outward appearances or through a setting in a public arena.

The *shadow* embodies personality qualities rejected by the ego as despicable. It is the most important representation of the personal unconscious, the sum of all those things we have deliberately forgotten and do not like about ourselves. In waking life the shadow is often projected onto those we despise. It typically emerges in the second half of life when the potential of the ego to realise its ambitions is tarnished by accumulated shortcomings. It also occurs through the excessive development of our strong-points. In the gospel of Luke, Martha (helping but distracted) is the shadow for her sister Mary (contemplative but lazy) (Lk 10:38-42). The spontaneous and wasteful Prodigal Son has as his shadow the dutiful but resentful elder brother (Lk 15:11-32).

The shadow is typically projected in dreams as an unattract-ive and uncouth character, a hateful person, a dangerous animal or demonic being. The figure may be depicted as hidden away in a basement or some dank outhouse. The shadow often appears malnourished reflecting the inattention given to this aspect of the personality. The dream shadow has the same gender as the dreamer since it refers to an element of the individual's person-ality. The dreamer's normal reaction to the shadow is one of fear. However, the shadow is really part of oneself and its en-gagement facilitates growth in maturity. We can learn as much from struggling with our dark side as we can from playing to our strengths. Jungians refer to the shadow as being 90% gold.

The *anima* is the feminine aspect of a man, while the *animus* is the corresponding personification of the masculine within a woman. These figures (together termed the *syzygy*) embody gender characteristics that are lacking in a man's or woman's conscious personality. Feminine consciousness is characterised by intimacy, but lacks the will to power. Men on the other hand are driven by ambition, but are typically insensitive. Becoming aware of the animus helps a woman to be more enterprising, while the anima furthers a man's sense of being-in-relationship.

As with the shadow, the syzygy is often projected in con-scious life. This is typically evident in the mutual attraction between a man and a woman, where each sees in the other something that is really hidden in themselves. The romantic aura will evaporate as soon as the projection is withdrawn and the other is seen as his or her true self. Ultimately we should be-friend our own 'invisible partner' for the sake of more genuine relations with the opposite gender.

In dreams the anima might appear as a beautiful woman

with a mysterious allure who guides the person to some hidden truth. The animus can be imaged as a paternal figure, a sports champion or a thug. In its various manifestations this encourages the woman to negotiate reality in a courageous, physical and decisive way. Over time, the anima/animus becomes, as the Latin word implies, a soul image or faculty of relationship with the archetypal aspects of the personality, especially the Self.

Jungian literature describes other gender specific archetypes which, like the syzygy, facilitate the dialogue between the conscious and the archetypal unconscious. The *puer aeternus* (eternal child) in a man and the *puella aeterna* (eternal maiden) in a woman, can be constellated in dreams by the contrasting experiences of a new beginning or being tied to a childhood state. On the other hand, the *senex* (wise old man) and *magna mater* (the great mother) are psychic personifications of protective wisdom. The playfulness in the puer is compensated by the call to responsibility in the senex. Conversely, the excessive seriousness in the senex is highlighted by the puer's spontaneity.

The *Self* (in German 'das Selbst'; literally, 'the itself') is the most central and mysterious of the archetypes. Of all the archetypes it is least contained by its image. It is presented by Jung in three ways. It can be the counterpoint of the ego, the voice of conscience, which gives consolation in times of difficulty (Acts 9:31) and challenge in times of comfort (Jn 16:13). Or, it is the archetype of wholeness, representing the totality of the cosmos, including the individual, as filled with the divine (Eph 1:23; 3:19). Thirdly, Jung equated the Self with the *imago Dei in homine*, the image of God indwelling the person (Rom 8; 2 Cor 4:4-6; Jn 15:26; 16:7-16).

The Self can be represented through dreams in a great variety of ways. Many of these images are projected in the Bible. It can be heard like a disembodied voice that is invisible and authoritative (Gen 15:12; 1 Sam 3:1-9). It is sometimes imaged by impersonal objects such as a courtyard (Ps 84:2, 10), a spring (Jn 7:38), a garden (Gen 2:8-14) or a cornerstone (1 Pet 2:4; 1 Cor 10:4). These settings are reminiscent of the sanctuary, a delimited space in which the divinity is present. The Self may also be represented by a diamond or rare stone (Mt 13:44-46). The divine presence may be associated with symbols such as a rock (Ps

42:9) or a mountain (Ex 19-20). In other cases the Self is depicted in dreams as a supraordinate personality like a king, a prophet, a saviour or a hero. When they occur in 'big' dreams such images are symbolic and connect the dreamer with the presence of God.

Jung frequently associated dreams featuring the Self with the *mandala*, a traditional Eastern aid to meditation. With their circular and symmetrical patterns these represent the nature of God as a circle whose centre is everywhere and circumference nowhere.[26] Jung also identified the spirals of Celtic art and the rose window of churches as mandalas. He conceived the depiction of the heavenly Jerusalem in the Book of Revelation (Rev 21:12-21) and the interior castle of St Teresa of Avila as architectural mandalas.

---

26. C. G. Jung, 'A Psychological Approach to the Dogma of the Trinity' (1948) CW 11, par. 229n. Here Jung refers to the medieval formula: 'Deus est circulus cuius centrum est ubique, circumferentia vero nusquam.'

Day 14: Jungian Dream Interpretation

At the heart of Jung's approach to dream analysis is a respect for the dream itself: 'So difficult is it to understand a dream that for a long time I have made it a rule, when someone tells me a dream and asks for my opinion, to say first of all to myself: "I have no idea what this dream means." After that I begin to examine the dream.'[27] While Sigmund Freud usually directed the interpretation with reference to the idea that dreams were disguised sexual wishes, Jung sought to treat the dream at face value. He opposed dream dictionaries, lists of typical images with prescribed meanings. These standardise the interpretation and fail to appreciate the personal context. Properly undertaken, dream analysis is a painstaking task.

Dreams are normally a reaction to the waking life of the dreamer. The same dream can have two entirely different meanings, depending on the identity of the dreamer. For example, both an old and a young man had a dream concerning a group of youths who were horse riding.[28] In both cases, the dreamer led the group and cleared the ditch while his companions fell from their mounts. In their conscious lives, the young dreamer had a cautious personality while the old man was a restless invalid. For the youth, this dream was a positive compensation, telling him that he ought to be more adventurous. For the elderly man, the dream compensated in a negative way, counselling him to be more careful.

Jung valued the role of the analyst's intuition in arriving at an interpretation. At times, his impatience and easy use of intuition made the dream analysis less than thorough. Robert

---

27. C. G. Jung, 'On the Nature of Dreams' (1945/1948) CW 8, par. 533.
28. C. G. Jung, 'Symbols and the Interpretation of Dreams' (1961) CW 18, par. 519.

Johnson describes an occasion when Jung 'took me into the garden and proceeded to give me a very long lecture on the meaning of my dream ... Non-directive counselling, indeed!'[29] In his letters, Jung all too readily interpreted the dreams of people who wrote to him, without being aware of their life-context. He was inclined to see archetypal material in dreams which might equally be looked upon as merely personal. However, in principle at least, Jung held that authentic dream analysis requires a lack of predisposition.

In the Jungian method, dream analysis consists of gathering *associations* and making *amplifications*. The dreamer provides personal associations, while the analyst amplifies the dream images to find links with cultural and religious motifs. The first of these steps relates each image to the situation of the dreamer. In looking for the patient's associations Jung would ask such questions as: 'What occurs to you in connection with that?' or, 'How do you mean that, what does that come from, what do you think about it?'[30] He would pay particular attention to the element of a dream that elicited an emotional response as this indicated the presence of a complex.

Jung contrasted his method of gathering the patient's associations with that of Freud. In Freud's method of 'free association' one reminiscence was used as the basis for the next and so on. This led the dreamer away from the dream in a zig-zag pattern. The Jungian approach, by contrast remains with the dream image. With Freud, the goal was to uncover the patient's unconscious thoughts in the psychoanalysis itself. Jung agreed that such an approach identified the complexes which lay behind the dream's manifest content. However, the dream might remain unexplained.

Most dreams refer to the conscious life of the individual. Images in the dream can either project aspects of the dreamer's own personality, or refer to important people and places in the life of the dreamer. In the case of Anna Maria, an eighteen year old English woman, Jung diagnosed a dominant mother as the

---

29. F. Jensen (ed), *C. G. Jung, Emma Jung and Toni Wolff: A Collection of Remembrances* (San Francisco: Analytical Psychology Club, 1982), 37-38.
30. C. G. Jung, *Memories, Dreams, Reflections*, 170.

cause of her anorexia.[31] She reported the dream of a female spider that directed traffic along the threads of a web. Her situation was further represented in a dream of being engulfed by a mountain shaped like two breasts. The woman's sense of independence began to grow once she recognised that her dreams were images for the excessive influence of her mother.

Personal associations take precedence in dreamwork. The second level of association, archetypal amplification, only becomes necessary when the dream images cannot be explained by the dreamer's life. Archetypal dreams spring from the collective level of the unconscious. While they are coloured by the individual context they seem to come from a different level of experience. Such dreams are typically set in an archaic region or time and possess an aura of mystery. They employ archetypal actors such as the *senex* and the *magna mater* which may not be recognisable from waking life. Such dreams are numinous and command the dreamer's attention.

Dreams involving the collective dimension of the unconscious are of much benefit. They connect individual concerns with the human condition as a whole. When an archetype is evident in a dream it can be elaborated with reference to cultural myths, fairy-tales and beliefs. These ancient projections of the archetypes still resonate with us today because they express an element of the psyche which is common to humanity in every time and place. For Christians, the Bible is the key source for archetypal spiritual truths. In discovering a link between a passage from scripture and a dream image, a contemporary personal story finds its place with that of God's people.

In some cases the dream itself refers to a passage of scripture. In a dream which Morton Kelsey reported to Jung, he and a fellow clergyman were going to hear a lecture to be delivered by Jung in Los Angeles.[32] Their car broke down *en route*. Dressed as a medic in the dream, Jung asked Kelsey to explain his late arrival and then said that it was easier for a minister to be committed to religion than a doctor.

---

31. V. Brome, *Jung. Man and Myth* (New York: Atheneum, 1978), 178-179.
32. C. G. Jung, 'To Rev. Morton T. Kelsey' (27 December 1958), *Letters*, Vol 2: 1951-1961. G. Adler and A. Jaffé (eds), (New Jersey: Princeton University Press, 1975).

In his comments on this dream Jung associated the phrase he had used in the dream with a saying of Jesus: 'It is easier for a camel to pass through the eye of a needle than for a rich man' (Lk 18:25). The dream implied that Kelsey was trusting in psychology, but that this means to salvation had let him down. Jung's analysis concluded with the following challenge: 'Why would you need to prefer to talk to a doctor since you are totally committed to a Soter (Saviour), the greatest of all healers?'

A dream interpretation is formulated at the conclusion of the process of gathering personal and archetypal associations. It can complement or compensate the conscious situation of the dreamer. Other dreams are prospective in orientation. However compensation is the most general principle. Jung would ask the dreamer: 'What conscious attitude does it compensate?'[33] An interpretation which does not confront a consciously held belief is probably inaccurate. This axiom reiterates the importance of a knowledge of the dreamer's lived situation.

Finally, the interpretation should be subject to verification. Every conclusion is regarded as a guess until one is found which 'clicks' with the dreamer. An outcome which is pointless should be reconsidered. An accurate analysis is likely to be consistent with previous or subsequent dreams. Another indicator of a valid interpretation is the fulfillment of the events anticipated by the dream. Where no interpretation can be made, the dreamwork at least serves as a reminder that life is a mystery to be lived rather than a puzzle which can be solved.

---

33. C. G. Jung, 'The Practical Use of Dream Analysis' (1934) CW 16, par. 330.

Theology

An angel of the Lord appeared in a dream. Mt 1:20

Day 15: Hebrew Scripture on Dreams

The Bible often refers to dreaming as a way of revealing God's presence and will. In the Book of Numbers a prophet's vocation is said to be given in a dream or vision (Num 12:5-8). However, whereas God spoke face to face with Moses, the lesser prophets did so in dreams (Num 12:6). Dreams are a less direct communication from God. Samuel equates the religious value of dreams with oracles and the sayings of a prophet (1 Sam 28:6). In this reference King Saul has been deprived of all three channels of spirituality.

The Book of Joel sees self-disclosure by God in dreams as a sign of the immediacy of divine blessing in the messianic age (Joel 3:1; cf Acts 2:17). The prophet Daniel states that dreams exist for the benefit of the dreamer so that the mystery of our inmost thoughts can be revealed by God (Dan 2:28-30). In other words, by accurately stating the truth of your personal situation, dreams bring a divine perspective to self-knowledge.

In the Old Testament Joseph, son of Jacob, is the pre-eminent 'man of dreams' (Gen 37:19). Some of his own dreams are reported (Gen 37:5-11) and he became a gifted dream interpreter during his captivity in Egypt (Gen 40-41). One night the Pharaoh dreamt of seven fat cows coming up the River Nile followed by seven lean cows which then ate the fat animals (Gen 41:1-4). In another dream, seven ears of corn on one stalk were devoured by a stalk with seven scanty ears of corn (Gen 41:5-7). Joseph interpreted these parallel dreams as a revelation of God's will for Egypt, that a cycle of plenty would be followed by famine (Gen 41:13-36). The analysis was accepted and Joseph was appointed governor to oversee the storage of surplus food during a time of plenty so that the subsequent years of famine would not lead to mass starvation (Gen 41:37-57).

The cultural meaning of these dream images helps explain

the logic of Joseph's interpretation. The number seven signified a complete cycle in the Jewish mind set. The cow was regarded as a sacred animal in Egypt, being particularly associated with fertility.

The prophet Daniel also became a gifted dream interpreter in the court of a gentile king (Dan 1:17, 5:11-12, 7:1). His ability to interpret dreams was a God-given gift (Dan 2:27-28). He was able to correctly understand Nebuchadnezzar's parallel dreams concerning the destruction of the Babylonian empire (Dan 2-4). Like Joseph in Genesis, Daniel was able to construe the pattern of future events from the dream. They both had privileged insight into the will of God, by accurately reading the signs available to them in the dreams of their rulers.

A critical evaluation of dream interpretation is also evident in Hebrew scripture. Whereas early Israel welcomed all religious dreams, the need for qualitative distinctions later became apparent. A cautious view was first taken in Deuteronomy where it is written that the dreamer of a heretical message should be executed (Deut 13:2-6). This text is really a condemnation of divination: the attempt to gain insight into hidden cosmic truths. Such knowledge is reserved, by right, to God alone. The censure in Deuteronomy was particularly directed against the influence of local Canaanite cults (Deut 12:29-30; 18:9-14) which featured dream sanctuaries. Jacob's dream of the ladder (Gen 28:10-22) bears some resemblance to precisely such a structure.

The prophets Jeremiah and Zechariah likewise disapproved the person who claimed insight into God's will through dreams (Jer 23:25-28; 27:9; Zech 10:2). For the Jew, fidelity to God, rather the receipt of astonishing insights from God, is the hallmark of genuine religion. However the *de facto* influence of spiritual dreamwork in ancient Jewish spirituality can be assumed, given the strength of these condemnations.

The Bible's Wisdom books, composed between the fifth and second centuries BC, are generally suspicious of the view that dreams can be vehicles for divine inspiration. The ephemeral character of the dream is noted in the Psalms (Ps 73:20; 90:5). The Book of Proverbs regards sleep as an occasion of laziness (Prov 6:4-9). Ecclesiastes says that dreams are a source of vanity and provoke idle worry (Eccl 5:2-7; cf Sir 40:5). On the other hand, sleep is seen as a gift from God (Ps 4:8; 127:2) and joy is likened to a dream (Ps 126:1). Even at night the Lord can visit and direct our hearts (Ps 17:3; Song 5:2). The Book of Ecclesiasticus distinguishes ordinary and God-sent dreams (Sir 34:1-8). This passage states that ordinary dreams, like Jung's 'little' dreams, do not merit serious reflection. Here there is a notable reference to the ability of the dream to complement the situation of the dreamer, thereby promoting self-knowledge (Sir 34:3). The passage is generally hostile to the interpretation of dreams and associates it with divination (Sir 34:4-5).

The Book of Job, which also belongs to Wisdom literature, highlights the critical Jewish attitude to dreams in contrast with that of the Gentiles. Job complains that God can terrify him in dreams (Job 7:14) and also refers to their insubstantial quality (Job 20:8). However, Elihu, one of Job's gentile consolers, asserts that God can open a person's ears to divine instruction in dreams (Job 33:15-18). The human being is distracted from God's speech in the conscious state, with all its hustle and bustle. The weakness of the ego during sleep increases mental sensitivity to the Word of God.

Apart from these explicit references, many other settings for divine revelation in the Bible are synonymous with the dreaming state. The Hebrew understanding of the term 'vision' intended a kind of interior seeing that is consistent with dreaming.[1] Scripture itself occasionally associates dreams with visions (Num 12:6; Joel 2:28-29; Job 20:8, 33:15). This link is particularly evident in the phrase 'vision of the night' (Job 20:8; Isa 29:7; Dan 7:2, 7, 13). It might be that the use of the term 'vision' distinguishes a religious dream from an ordinary dream. In using the word 'vision' the biblical writer wanted to denote the divine content of a particular dream. It cannot be ascertained if these revelations were actually dreams. The Bible focuses on the content of the vision rather than providing a sustained reflection on its medium.

In most references to dreams in Hebrew scripture the meaning of the dream is clear. God imparts a message (Gen 20:3,

---

1. S. Legasse and M. Dulaey, 'Sognes-Rêves,' in M. Viller et al (eds), *Dictionnaire de spiritualité ascétique et mystique* 14 (Paris: Beauchesne, 1990), col. 1058.

31:11) and the dreamer responds (Gen 20:5, 31:17). Thus before the battle of Nicanor, Judas Maccabeus encouraged his men by telling them a dream, 'worthy of belief' which foresaw victory (2 Macc 15:11-16). Only in the Joseph and Daniel cycles is dream analysis applied and in these cases is required solely by Gentiles such as Nebuchadnezzar or Pharaoh. In contrast with the confusion of the dream experts at the pagan royal courts (Gen 41:8; Dan 4:4-5), the interpretations offered by Jews are clear and accurate. A sense of privileged access to divine revelation is evident in the Hebrew self-concept.

One notable exception to this observation occurs in the Book of Judges. Gideon overheard a Midianite soldier sharing his dream of a cake of barley that tumbled into their camp, overturning the staff tent (Judg 7:12-15). A companion soldier interpreted the cake as the sword of Gideon and the collapse of the tent as the defeat of the Midianites. Gideon accepted this analysis as an omen of victory. This is the only occasion in the Bible when a Gentile is presented as capable of accurate dream interpretation.

Day 16: Christian Scripture on Dreams

The Greek word for 'dream' (*onar*) is used just seven times in the New Testament, with five of these references in the infancy narrative of Matthew. In the first instance, an angel appears to Joseph to explain Mary's pregnancy (Mt 1:20). The dream told him that Mary's conception of Jesus was by the Holy Spirit and that he should go ahead with their marriage. The couple had been engaged to each other and Mary's apparent infidelity would have invoked severe penalties under the Law of Moses (Deut 22:20-25). Joseph's decision to stand by Mary (Mt 1:24-25) demonstrates an acceptance of the authority of dreaming as an expression of God's will.

The dream was an apt vehicle for Joseph to receive the news of Mary's pregnancy. Dreams characteristically assert the viability of the scientifically impossible. A psychologist might argue that this dream was Joseph's reaction to the news of Mary's pregnancy. His unconscious invented a miraculous explanation for the event, out of a desire to deny the obvious conclusion that she had betrayed their engagement. Most biblical theologians understand the dream as Matthew's attempt to come to terms with the inexplicable. The virginal conception of Jesus, while clearly stated in tradition, can only be accepted in faith.

In the second dream God directly warns the Magi to avoid King Herod and return to their own country (Mt 2:12). The third dream has an angel telling Joseph to flee with his family to Egypt and so avoid the persecution of Herod (Mt 2:13). In the fourth dream, Joseph is told that Herod is dead and Israel can once again be their home (Mt 2:19). However, in the fifth dream, an angel warned Joseph against settlement in Judea which was now ruled by Herod's son (Mt 2:22). The Holy Family then settled in the northerly province of Galilee. In the only other incident of a dream in the gospels, Pontius Pilate's wife reports to her husband the distress she suffered in a dream on account of the impending passion of Jesus (Mt 27:19). All of these incidents show an appreciation that divine communication can occur in dreams. Each of the dreams occurs at times of personal turmoil or discernment and offers practical guidance. Matthew wanted to show the activity of God on Jesus' behalf at all stages of his life.

The Greek phrasing normally used by Matthew for 'an angel of the Lord appeared in a dream' (Mt 1:20; 2:13, 19), dates from the time of the gospel's composition (70-80 AD).[2] It has the tone of a formula or literary device rather than history. Matthew's references to dreams are not paralleled by Luke, the author of the other infancy narrative (Lk 2). Matthew uses the dreams to reconcile the tradition of Jesus' birth in Bethlehem (Judea) with his upbringing in Nazareth (Galilee). Luke would explain these facts with a Roman census (Lk 2:1-2). For Matthew, the Egyptian exile served to highlight Jesus as the new Moses, who had also come out of Egypt (Mt 2:15). At no point does Luke place the baby Jesus in Egypt. Such inconsistencies point to the essence of the gospels as theology rather than history. Even though the accounts appear factual, Matthew and Luke really wanted to proclaim the nature of Jesus, rather than give an historical account of his birth. In any case the incarnation was a supernatural event that lies beyond human comprehension. However, Matthew clearly assumed that dreaming could be acceptably viewed as a means by which God can communicate with humanity.

There is just one other use of the word 'dream' in the New Testament. In the Acts of the Apostles, Peter quotes the prophet Joel's reference to dreams in the messianic age (Acts 2:17, cf Joel 3:1-5). Joel's prediction of a new age when 'your young men shall see visions and your old men shall dream dreams' has, for Peter, been ushered in by Jesus.

There are many indirect references to dreaming in the New Testament. Insofar as dreams can be associated with the 'vision' (Acts 9:10), 'trance' (Acts 10:10, 11:5) or the 'vision of the night' (Acts 16:9-10, 18:9; 27:23) further evidence for the religious role

---

2. A Oepke, 'Onar' in G. J. Botterweck and H. Ringgren (eds) *Theological Dictionary of the Old Testament* 5 (Grand Rapids, MI: Eerdmans Publishing Co, 1986), 235.

of dreaming can be found. These citations continue Matthew's notion of the practical guidance offered by dreams. For example in Acts 16, Paul redirected the course of his mission to Macedonia, having been beckoned to do so in a night vision (Acts 16:9-10). Likewise he was prepared for the journey to Rome by an appearance of the Lord during the night (Acts 23:11).

In three of Joseph's dreams in Matthew and in one of Paul's night visions, the divine message is given by an angel (Mt 1:20, 2:13, 19; Acts 27:23). This continues the Old Testament association between dream-visions and angels (Zech 1:7-9). Both the Hebrew term *malak* and the Greek *aggelos* suggest a literal translation of the word 'angel' as 'messenger'. It was not until the later Old Testament period that the role of angels was affirmed by sections of Judaism, most notably by the Pharisees. This was because of a developing sense of God's transcendence in Jewish theology. While the earliest writings described divine revelation as involving the personal appearance of the Lord (Gen 15:12-13; 20:3), angels later came to be seen as the representatives of God's message. In the Book of Daniel the angel Gabriel is regarded as the bearer of visions to humanity (Dan 9:21-22).

The transition from the Old to the New Testament is marked by a reduced interest in dreams as a vehicle of revelation. While Christian scripture does not deny the spiritual significance of dreams there are fewer references to that belief in comparison with first-century near-Eastern culture. Dream criticism was then an academic discipline that ranked alongside medicine and astrology. The literary genre of the dream dictionary, epitomised by the *Oneirocritica* of Artemidorus (140-180 AD) is not to be found in the Bible.

In contrast to many Old Testament dreams, the New Testament reports the dream narrative as it takes place rather than after the dreamer awakes. This suggests that Christian scripture is merely interested in the content of the message and there is a marked absence of reflection on dreaming as the vehicle of that revelation. There are no references to dreams in the life of Jesus and the interpretation of dreams, as distinguished from dream reportage, is entirely absent from the New Testament. This may be due to the Christian assertion that God has been clearly manifested in Jesus Christ, effectively making redundant all other means of revelation. The Spanish mystic St John of the Cross (1542-1591) would argue that God-sent visions were only common in Old Testament times because direct revelation through Jesus Christ had not yet been established.[3] There was, according to this view, a divine dispensation granted in the biblical era, one which no longer applies.

Taken as a whole, the Bible has an ambivalent attitude to the religious significance of dreaming. On the one hand, dreams are an expression of the irrational depths of human nature and are deceitful and insignificant (Job 20:8; Ps 73:20; Isa 29:7-8; Sir 34:1-8). The Book of Deuteronomy prohibits the professional practice of dream interpretation (Deut 13:2-6). On the other hand, scripture clearly affirms that God or God's messengers may communicate with the human being in a dream (Gen 20:3; 28-12-15; 37:5-10; Num 12:6; Ps 17:3; Mt 1:20, 2:13, 19). Apart from the references to Joseph's dreams in Matthew, the New Testament has a taciturn attitude to the spiritual relevance of dreams.

---

3. John of the Cross, *Ascent of Mount Carmel*, 2.22.3.

Day 17: Patrick of Ireland

The use of dreams in ancient Christian sources can be divided into two categories: those which simply report dreams as divine messages and theological reflection on the meaning of dreams. Patrick of Ireland (c. 390-c. 460) is a good example of an author who directly reported his dreams. His short autobiography, the *Confession*, is the earliest Christian writing from Britain or Ireland and a rich source of spiritual theology.

Patrick grew up in Roman Britain towards the end of the fourth century. His home country had become vulnerable to Irish pirates even before the withdrawal of Roman troops to mainland Europe in 407. It was during one such raid that sixteen year old Patrick was captured and sold into slavery in Ireland. At this time in Christian Britain and Gaul, a form of monasticism inspired by the strict lifestyle of the Egyptian desert fathers had developed. The voluntary heroism of the Celtic monks over-stressed the role of willpower in the divine-human relationship. The monk who sponsored this heresy, Pelagius, spread his ideas in Britain before moving to Europe, not later than the year 400. By contrast the church councils at Nicea (325), Constantinople III (381) and Ephesus (431) retained a concept of salvation as a free gift from God, not one merited by our own efforts.

Patrick received his formal religious formation in Gaul and was sent to Ireland by Pope Celestine I about the year 432. The anti-Pelagian tone of his mission is the key to understanding the spirituality of the *Confession*. Patrick attributes his success to God rather than his own work: 'It was the gift of God.' (*Confession*, 62). He regarded night dreams as an important source of divine assistance.

There are seven distinct dreams or dream-like visions reported in the *Confession*. In the first, during his initial captivity in Ireland, Patrick heard a voice telling him that he would soon return to Britain. A little later he 'heard a voice during sleep' to say that his ship for Gaul was ready (*Confession* 17). The fact that this dream prompted a walk of two hundred miles demonstrates Patrick's confidence in its divine inspiration. During a second captivity in Ireland, Patrick received a 'divine message' at night which accurately revealed the duration of his imprisonment (*Confession* 21). Later, having returned to Britain, he 'saw a night vision' in which a man called Victoricus brought him countless letters from Ireland (*Confession* 23). As he read the letters, Patrick could hear the people with whom he had lived in Ireland pleading for his return. Itself like a letter from the depths of his being, this dream was foundational to Patrick's vocation. The call back to Ireland was confirmed on another night and he awoke 'full of joy' (*Confession* 24).

Subsequently, Patrick encountered much opposition to his ambition of becoming a missionary in Ireland. At a time when he was threatened with disgrace owing to the betrayal of a friend, a 'vision of the night' assured him of God's support (*Confession* 29). The voice of God then disapprovingly spelt out the name of his accuser. As with Jacob's dream of the ladder (Gen 28:10-18), this one assured Patrick of God's support at a time of fraternal rivalry.

The *Confession* uses two distinct phrases to introduce dreams. In the dreams where something is seen, the biblical expression 'a vision of the night' is employed (*Confession* 23, 29; cf Dan 7:2, 7, 13). In other places the text introduces the dream narrative with the phrase '*responsum divinum*' (*Confession* 17, 21, 29). This implies that Patrick received his dreams as a 'divine response' to his situation and especially his prayer. In the first dream, the promise of liberation came as a result of prayer and fasting offered during captivity. This suggests that Patrick asked God to provide solutions to his problems through dreams.

Supernatural presence is strongly personalised in the dreams of paragraphs 20 and 25. The first of these has the atmosphere of a nightmare:

> That same night when I was asleep, Satan assailed me violently, a thing I shall remember as long as I shall be in this body. And he fell upon me like a huge rock and I could not

stir a limb. But whence came it into my mind, ignorant as I am, to call upon Helias? And meanwhile I saw the sun rise in the sky, and while I was shouting 'Helias! Helias!' with all my might, suddenly the splendour of that sun fell upon me and immediately freed me of all misery. And I believe that I was sustained by Christ my Lord and that His Spirit was even then crying out on my behalf. (*Confession* 20)

This dream took place as Patrick wandered through Gaul following his escape from captivity in Ireland. The day before he had refused to eat the food which his travelling companions had offered to a pagan god. This set the scene for the dream image of conflict with Satan. In response to the entrapment by the devil, Patrick cried out the name of Helias and then the sun rose. This part can be seen as a confusion between the Latin words for Elijah and the Greek sun god Helios.[4] The sun-god had a chariot and the prophet Elijah was taken up to heaven in a fiery chariot (2 Kings 2:11). The Celts were worshippers of the sun and Patrick used this play on words to appeal that Christ was the true light ('*Christus sol verus*', *Confession* 60).

In Jungian psychology, the dialogue between a personification of the dreamer and other aspects of the dreamer's life is a typical dream mechanism. In this case the *dramatis personae* are Patrick, Satan and Christ. Satan represents the *shadow* side of all that is Christian. It is normal for the dream-ego to flee from this character. However, ultimately, its confrontation marks growth in maturity. The dream both expressed Patrick's experience of evil and reminded him that he could stand firm in the knowledge that he had been saved by Christ.

In paragraph twenty-five Patrick reported that one night he saw Christ 'praying in me, and I was as it were within my body, and I heard him above him, that is, over the inward man, and there he prayed mightily with groanings.' In this case Patrick's ego was being observed by Patrick the dreamer in a situation akin to an out of body experience. He was witnessing the prayer-life of Christ within him. He then quoted St Paul: 'The

---

4. L. Bieler (ed and tr), *The Works of St Patrick. St Secundinus Hymn on St Patrick*, [Ancient Christian Writers 17] (New York: Newman Press, 1953), 84

Spirit himself expresses our plea in a way that could never be put into words.' (*Confession* 25; Rom 8:26) Patrick interprets the dream with a theology of prayer which sees the believer as a sharer in the life of the Trinity. All Christian prayer re-enacts the attitude of Christ before the Father, with the Spirit as the bond of love between them. This dream powerfully dramatised Patrick's belief in God's indwelling presence.

Readers of the *Confession* will find themselves demythologising a saint known for his miraculous powers in Irish folklore. This process can be extended to the *Confession* itself by regarding many of the divine revelations it narrates as dreams rather than overtly supernatural phenomena. While we are impressed by his extraordinary visions, Patrick simply appreciated the spiritual implications of his dreams.

Day 18: Christian Tradition on Dreams

Of the ancient writers who provide theological reflection on dreaming, Tertullian's contribution has already been summarised (Day 7). The next significant reference in Christian tradition was from the Desert Fathers, those early monks who practised a spirituality of *fuga mundi* (flight from the world). One of the first, Athanasius of Alexandria (293/5-373), believed that dreams allowed demons to act more freely on a person.[5] They tempt the sleeping Christian with the possibility of foreknowledge, something which properly belongs to God. Another, John Cassian (c. 365-435), discussed whether a dream which provoked a nocturnal emission excluded a monk from receiving communion.[6] He concluded that the monk could still receive the Eucharist because such dreams are inflicted by the devil and fall outside the monk's own responsibility.

St Jerome (c. 347-c. 420) was ambiguous on the question of divine revelation in dreams. He discerned his vocation to be a theologian in a dream which imagined him brought before a tribunal.[7] The judge demanded to know his identity. Jerome replied that he was a Christian. However, the judge accused him of being a disciple of the philosopher Cicero and not Christ. He then took an oath never again to possess secular books. The dream inspired Jerome to become a hermit and biblical scholar. However, his influential *Vulgate* translation of the Bible into Latin misinterpreted some texts (notably Lev 19:26 and Deut 18:10) as a prohibition of the observation of dreams.[8] An accurate rendering condemns divination but does not refer to oneiro-

---

5. Athanasius, *Life of Anthony*, 34-35.
6. John Cassian, *Conferences*, 22.
7. Jerome, Letter 22 (To Eustochium), 30.3-5.
8. M. T. Kelsey, *Dreams: The Dark Speech of the Spirit. A Christian Interpretation* (New York: Doubleday, 1968), 151-159.

mancy, the use of dreams for that purpose. This mistake encouraged the theological prohibition of any form of dream interpretation in subsequent centuries.

The work *De insomniis (On Dreams)* by Bishop Synesius of Cyrene (c. 370-414) marked a high point of classical thought on dreams. Synesius saw the capacity for imagination, so characteristic of dreams, as a means for divine communication. In contrast with dry factual instruction, God imparts knowledge in dreams by delight. Synesius appreciated that the interpretation of a dream belongs to the dreamer and so criticised the prescribed meanings given in dream dictionaries. This work describes the ability of dreams to predict the future. The explanation offered was based on Plato's theory of forms. The improved sensory capacity of the soul in sleep allowed insight into the timeless forms that are beyond physical reality. Synesius claimed that the analysis of dreams should not be reserved to dream experts. He advised preparation for sleep with prayer and the use of a 'night book' to record dreams.

The writings of St Augustine (354-430) both reported dreams and sometimes reflected on their spiritual significance. Akin to Jung's 'big' and 'little' dream, he distinguished ordinary dreams (*phantasie*) from inspired dreams (*ostensiones*). In the *Confession*, his mother uses her intuition to discern the divine or natural origins of the dream.[9] Her concerns for Augustine's future had provoked natural dreams which she did not consider worth recounting to him. For Augustine, dream narratives resemble scripture in being replete with symbolic meaning.[10] Being imaginative rather than literal reproductions of memory they can facilitate the perception of hidden spiritual meanings behind everyday objects.

In the East, Gregory of Nyssa (c. 335-394) emphasised the physiological causes of dreams in Chapter Thirteen of *On the Making of Man* entitled: 'A Rationale for Sleep, Yawning and Dreams'. He held that while the rational mind dominated over the functions of nutrition and sensation during consciousness, this order is reversed in sleep since rest is required for the digestion

---

9. Augustine, *Confession*, 6.13. Cf S. Legasse and M. Dulaey, 'Sognes-Rêves,' cols. 1061-1062.
10. Augustine, *The Literal Meaning of Genesis*, 10.25.42.

of food. For Gregory, dreams were typically framed by the memories of the day, the nutritional condition of the body and the character of the dreamer. He believed that some dreams could be a communication from God.

Pope Gregory the Great (540-604) took a negative stance on dream interpretation. In a section of the *Dialogues*, he listed six causes of dreams: the state of the body, the preceding day's events, the devil, the sleeper's thoughts in conjunction with the devil, a revelation by God and the sleeper's thoughts in conjunction with divine revelation.[11] Gregory emphasised the physical causes and illusory character of dreams. While he conceded that some dreams come from God, the difficulty in discerning a dream's origin made them generally untrustworthy. Only people with the calibre of the Old Testament prophets could interpret dreams correctly.

By the late Middle Ages we find fewer references to dreams in Christian literature. A most influential theologian, Thomas Aquinas (c.1225-1274) cited the biblical evidence which affirmed the spiritual role of dreams but chose to highlight those texts which condemned the practice of dream analysis. Aquinas emphasised the physiological and physical dimensions of dreams. Internally, dreams come from the sleeper's personal preoccupations or the condition of the body. Externally, dreams can be triggered by the surroundings of the dreamer or by a spiritual cause. The supernatural influence was sometimes demonic and 'sometimes referable to God, who reveals certain things to men in their dreams by the ministry of the angels.'[12] For Thomas, the deliberate use of dreams to obtain spiritual gifts was unlawful, being a form of divination. Dreams which carry a divine communication occurred spontaneously as a gift from God and should not be sought out.

Jerónimo Gracián, the confessor of Teresa of Avila (1515-1582), listed dreams as the tenth item in his twelve ways of the Spirit.[13] He distinguished three types of dreams. Firstly, there were dreams of a physiological origin. These were to be disregarded. Secondly, he held that some dreams were inspired by

---

11. Gregory the Great, *Dialogues*, 4.50.
12. T. Aquinas, *Summa Theologica*, II Q.95 Art. 6.
13. J. Gracián, *Peregrinación de Anastasio*, Obras 3, Dialogo 5: 'Sueños'.

angels, as exemplified by those of Joseph in Matthew's gospel. Thirdly, there are dreams that come from the devil. These characteristically involved sensuality and were to be resolutely rebutted.

In 1598 the Jesuit Benedictus Pererius published a book on oneirology.[14] This work listed four causes of dreams: food, emotions, the devil offering foreknowledge or sexual stimulation and fourthly, dreams sent by God. For Pererius, the majority of dreams were completely valueless. While anyone can potentially receive a communication from God in a dream, the counsel of the wise was needed to uncover an authentic divine message. This help was necessary due to the obscurity of dreams and their possibly diabolical origins. The discernment of dreams, he held, is itself a divine gift.

In short many Christian authors, following the biblical lead, recorded dreams and commented on the spiritual significance of dreaming. A substantial vein of tradition has been wary of spiritual dreamwork because of the purely personal causes of most dreams or the potential for demonic influence during sleep. This opinion grew with the passage of time. By the nineteenth century, the study of dreams, then neglected by theology, was taken up by the new science of psychology and became a thoroughly secular discipline. However, the work of Carl Jung restored an appreciation for a spiritual dimension in oneirology.

---

14. B. Pererius, *De Magia; De Observatione Somniorum et de Divinatione Astrologica*, (Coloniae Agrippinae: apud Ioannem Gymnicum, 1598).

Day 19: Does God Still Speak in Dreams?

Christianity sees Jesus as the fullness of God's self-revelation. Jesus' life on earth, his identity as Son of God and the record of that event, gives revelation primarily an historical, supernatural and public character. St John of the Cross and others wrote that God spoke in dreams only before Christ. Faith is now to be lived through study, action and prayer based on the gospel and the person of Jesus. However, on reflection, each of the three perspectives on revelation still allows for an understanding of divine communication in dreams.

Revelation Historical and Ongoing

The Christian faith does not just have a past, but was shaped through historical events concerning the life, death and resurrection of Jesus Christ. The apostles of Jesus directly witnessed the revelation of God in person (1 Jn 1:1-3) whereas all subsequent followers do so by faith. Their witness is contained in scripture and tradition. It has been entrusted to the church, not as a series of dogmas to be literally reproduced, but as something unfolding. The church listens for 'signs of the times', ways that God's Spirit is speaking today. However, while tradition should not be petrified, neither can it be updated at the expense of altering the faith. All current forms of revelation are said to be dependent on the foundational event. Revelation is closed in the sense that Christ, the fullness of revelation, has already been presented. Ongoing revelation actualises the Christ event but does not contribute to its content. It is the Spirit which guides the followers of Jesus toward a fuller disclosure of God in their lives (Jn 16:12-14). Dreams which lead to this fuller unveiling of God can be considered part of the ongoing movement of God's Spirit in the world.

Revelation Supernatural and Natural

God's ways are revealed to all humanity by natural means such as the use of reason, friendship and beauty. However, the church teaches that God is primarily made known in supernatural ways.[15] These provide links to the life of God which exceed the possibilities provided by the five senses. The supernatural is evident in private revelations and miracles, both of which go beyond the laws of nature. It is epitomised in Christ, who was fully divine as well as fully human.

Dreaming is clearly a natural process. It exceeds the laws of time and space only in the dreamer's imagination. It is thereby a less important vehicle for God's self-revelation. However, Christians understand the orders of nature and supernature to be in communion rather than confrontation. God is not wholly transcendent and the natural world has an innate tendency toward the Creator through the presence of the Holy Spirit. As naturally occurring phenomena, dreams too can be potential sources for God's action in our lives.

Revelation Public and Private

Theology distinguishes between public and private revelation to account for the times in which God's will is still made known to individuals. While the fullness of revelation took place in Jesus and is transmitted by the public record of his life, private revelations have continued to occur. Exemplary incidents have included the divine communications to St Hildegarde (1098-1179), St Bridget of Sweden (1303-1373) and to St Margaret Mary Alacoque (1647-1690) at Paray-le-Monial. The Marian apparitions at Lourdes (1858), Knock (1879), Fatima (1917), and Banneux (1933) constitute another class of these special revelations. Such events have a moral and spiritual rather than doctrinal content. They add nothing new to the faith, yet they are helpful in making it more vital. In particular, private revelations are effective in compensating a spirituality based on dry academic study.

Theology traditionally conceives three types of private revelations.[16] The *visio sensibilis* is perceived by the bodily senses. It

15. Vatican II, *Dei verbum*, 3-6.
16. J. Ratzinger, 'Theological Commentary' in Congregation for the Doctrine of the Faith, *The Message of Fatima* (Libreria Editrice Vaticana, 2000), 36-38.

normally involves an apparition received in the waking state and is accessible to all who are present. The vision on the church gable in Knock was of this order. The *visio imaginativa* is an interior perception which concerns the recipient's mental consciousness. Such was the case at Lourdes and Fatima since not everyone present at the revelatory events received the same insights as the visionaries. The *visio intellectualis* is an intuitive knowledge, which affects neither the exterior nor interior senses. This is the spiritual vision of the great mystics such as John of the Cross, an experience of being-with-God that is without images.

In both 'sensible' and 'imaginative' visions a human element is involved in the perception of the supernatural. Private revelations of these types are children of their time, conditioned by the language and images available to the recipient. So the supernatural origin of a private revelation might not always be evident, but remain hidden under a natural guise. In the *visio imaginativa*, God communicates through the person's interior thoughts. This is the way that dreams might be adopted by God as a means of divine communication.

In an imaginative vision which authentically involves a divine communication something more than the personal dimensions of a dream should be expected. There would have to be a real perception of the transcendent within consciousness. Private revelations are considered to be extremely rare. They carry a message that is relevant to the church and are normally accompanied by a miracle. Dreams, by contrast, regularly occur, are natural in origin and usually personal in scope. However, to deny the possibility of revelation in dreams is to restrict God's freedom for self-manifestation. It is possible for God to speak to individuals in dreams as once was the case in the Bible.

A contemporary theology of revelation emphasises that both God and the human being are involved in the process. A loving God does not force to be heard, but awaits our attentiveness (1 Sam 3:1-21). An understanding of Jesus as God's Word (Jn 1:1-18) presupposes a listening disposition on the part of the disciple. The revelation that might be perceived as a dramatic unveiling of God is probably a personal awakening to some truth about God that has already been publically revealed. While the church claims that the fullness of revelation has already been established in Christ, each generation and individual still needs to discover that truth.

Christian spirituality traditionally links self-knowledge and our ability to experience God. As St Augustine prayed: 'God ever constant, let me know myself that I may know you.'[17] Our faith relationship with God, like every relationship, demands a level of self-awareness in order for it to function in an authentic way. The sense of personal identity gained from dreamwork can enhance this process. The insight into the interior life provided by dreams helps us uncover the truth about ourselves and brings us closer to the truth about God, whose Spirit dwells in the depths of human nature (Rom 8:14-16).

The subjective quality of dreams suggests that they are of value to the individual rather than the church. Dreams are concerned with personal guidance, whereas the theology of revelation focuses on the nature of God. While dreams may be a source of religious experience, Christian revelation, as such, is found in Jesus Christ. Yet faith in God is also personal. While dreams may no longer play a role in divine self-manifestation as such, they do 'open our ears' to God's voice (Job 33:15-18). Insofar as dreams reveal the correct meaning and direction of life, they coincide with the divine plan and make us more disposed to God's presence.

---

17. 'Deus semper idem, noverim me, noverim te', Augustine, *Soliloquies*, 2.1.

Day 20: The Image of God in Dreams

Our understanding of divine revelation in dreams is based on a person's sensitivity to God's presence rather than a dramatic intervention. However, the suggestion that we use an imaginative process like dreaming to encounter God runs the risk of making God a product of our own thinking. It was for this reason that Jung's description of God, based on his experience of the God-archetype (the Self) in dreams, at times differs sharply from the Christian depiction.

Jung wholeheartedly agreed with Rudolf Otto's association of spirituality with *numinosity*.[18] The numinous is a dynamic agency, outside human willpower which seizes a person. St Paul's blinding encounter with Christ on the road to Damascus is a good example (Acts 9:1-20). The numinous delivers a *mysterium tremendum et fascinans,* a sensation of being swept away gently or violently that is accompanied by feelings of dread as well as charm. Without such experience religion becomes stale and boring, just an intellectual exercise. For Jung, a religious dream is principally identified by its numinosity. Such dreams typically inspire awe and wonder. They link a person directly to the spiritual sphere.

In Jung's view, the church's teaching authority (the *Magisterium*) plays a positive role by censoring the numinous and defining objective standards for spirituality. Such control parallels the function of the conscious in relation to the unconscious. However, religious codes ultimately cannot substitute for something best known interiorly and personally. Jung gave precedence to personal or primary religious experience over any objective or secondary reflection on the event.

Organised religion contains numinous experiences within an

---

18. R. Otto, *The Idea of the Holy* (Oxford: University Press, 1923), 1-15.

institutional framework. Ideally, it strives for a form of contain-
ment that allows for personal experience. As such the charismat-
ic and hierarchical elements of the church can function in a complementary manner.

In the history of theology, the influence of Thomas Aquinas
is held responsible for reducing faith to a series of statements
about God which could be examined by reason. The sense of
revelation as personal encounter with God, so evident in the
Bible, was consequently lost. Aquinas' so-called *propositional*
model of revelation culminated with the First Vatican Council
(1869-1870). Another theological trend of the nineteenth century,
modernism, reacted against the tendency to rationalise spirituality and retrieved the biblical model of faith as a direct experience
of God.

With the Second Vatican Council (1962-1965) something of a
rapprochement between these two approaches occurred. The
Council developed a dynamic understanding of revelation as
God's loving address to humanity.[19] Faith is more than the intellectual reception of religious truths and involves a personal relationship with the divine. However, the Council equally taught
that the Word of God as expressed in the Bible and tradition remains the definitive point of reference for spiritual experience.

Jung did not accept Christ as the fullness of revelation. He
held that a church-based relationship with Christ can all too easily substitute for a personal encounter with the divine. He pointed out that Christians tend to focus on the historical and objective Jesus rather than the current and subjective ways in which
the presence of the God can happen in the believer today.

In Jungian psychology, God is typically manifested in
dreams by images of integrity, unity and wholeness such as the
mandala. These circular images are expressions of God as the all-
encompassing ground of reality. Dreams thus reveal God as a
complexio oppositorum which contains all spiritual experience,
evil as well as good.

In *Answer to Job* (1954) and elsewhere, Jung even went so far
as to suggest that God is properly understood as a quaternity,
rather than a trinity, and that the devil is the 'missing fourth' of
God. In his reading of the Book of Job, Jung understands

19. Vatican II, *Dei verbum* 2.

Yahweh's indifference to Job's misfortunes as an accurate reflection of God's dark side. He explained the history of salvation as God's discovery of the feminine principle (the *anima*) in Sophia, the Wisdom of God. The Word became flesh and suffered on the cross to make amends for Yahweh's previous insensitivity to creation. This is a reversal of Christian theology: Jung holds that it is God rather than mankind that needed redemption.

Jung's theology of a quaternitarian God has provoked strident opposition. Critics have likened his position to the Manichean heresy, which made both good and evil into rival supernatural forces. In the Christian understanding of revelation there is only one God, whose nature is love (1 Jn 4:8). The inclusion of evil in the Godhead is abhorrent to Christianity. An orthodox theology teaches that evil detracts from rather than adds to godliness.

Jung claimed that his image of God was based on experience rather than revealed truths about the nature of God. His approach allows human concerns to determine the image of God. Religious dreams do indeed frequently portray the Lord as vengeful and terrifying. Likewise, the experience of tragedy, whether personal or natural, is often attributed to God's indifference or anger at human shortcomings. In primitive religions this led to the practice of ritual sacrifices to appease divine wrath. The Christian faith, with its emphasis of the otherness of God and the gratuity of salvation, represents an evolution from such a primordial spirituality. God's absolute goodness and care for creation is a cornerstone of the Bible and Christian faith. Yet God's ways are not our ways (Isa 55:9). In the Christian understanding, evil remains in God's kingdom as a mystery to be pondered rather than as a reflection of God's identity (Mt 13:24-30). The best conclusion to the problem of evil is that God's is an undefended power.

The spirituality consequent to Jung's theology conceives goodness and sin as existing in mutual relationship: 'There is no good that cannot produce evil and no evil than cannot produce good.'[20] He highlighted those elements of tradition which counselled an engagement with the shadow. Jesus did indeed advise

---

20. C. G. Jung, *Psychology and Alchemy* (1935/1953) CW 12, par. 36.

his disciples to come to terms with the adversary (Mt 5:25) as he himself did in the desert (Mt 4:1-11). While the theological image of God as the supreme good (the *summum bonum*) founds a spirituality of perfectionism (Mt 5:48), many contemporary Christians prefer Jung's suggestion that holiness is wholeness. Just as the human psyche is lopsided if it fails to face its shadow, so will Christian spirituality be incomplete without a more subtle response to the problem of evil. In the words of the Easter Vigil liturgy, sin can be a *felix culpa* (happy fault) by which a person turns toward God in deeper faith. Evil is routed not so much by condemnation and repression as through understanding, compassion and redemption.

A perfectionist spirituality risks divorcing the believer from the human condition and actually empowers evil through a denial of its existence. However, while an individual can paradoxically grow in perfection through the struggle with darkness this point cannot be seen as a reflection of God's nature. An authentic image of God is not only based on experience, but also transcends our limited horizons.

Day 21: Signs of the Kingdom in Dreams

The phrase 'kingdom of God' is central to the New Testament. In the Our Father it is described as a realm in which God's will is done as much on earth as it is in heaven (Mt 6:10; Lk 11:2). Jesus of Nazareth preached an imminent kingdom and Christians acclaim him as its bearer. A lived relationship with Christ acknowledges his role as king and extends his reign in the world. Today some of the classic tenets of kingdom theology will be compared with dream processes.

An Event, Not a Place. In the New Testament the kingdom is an event, rather than a territory with measurable boundaries. The Greek phrase *'basileia tou theou'* (kingdom of God) suggests a reign or power rather than a physical entity. God's kingdom is the rule of relatively intangible qualities such as truth, holiness, justice, love and peace. Dreaming too is not so much a concrete reality as a state of being that is powerful yet difficult to determine. Dreams are something to be experienced as they occur and cannot really be quantified according to laws of time and space. The analysis and interpretation of dreams, like the institutionalising of God's reign, somewhat reduces the strength of the original experience.

Already and Not Yet. In Christian scriptures the kingdom of God is both immediate and yet not fully realised. The future kingdom predicted by the Hebrew prophets has now come to pass in Jesus (Mk 1:15). However, God's reign has not yet fully arrived, as evidenced by the suffering and injustice which persists. St Augustine described this world as a *regio dissimilitudinis*, a holy place which has been alienated from God by sin.[21] Dreams too are a 'land of unlikeness', where there is both connection and discontinuity with waking reality. The possibilities

21. Augustine, *Confession*, 7.10.

envisioned by dreams are experienced as 'now' and yet are also merely an echo of some other reality. Archetypal dreams in particular feel as if they originate in a sphere that is not fully part of the present world.

Reversal of Status. In God's kingdom the first will be last and the last first (Mk 10:31). The mighty will be taken down from their thrones and made to experience vulnerability (Lk 1:51-53). Conversely those who weep, are persecuted and are poor find themselves 'blessed' (Mt 5:3-12; Lk 6:20-26). Dreams provide a platform for such reversal of status through their compensatory function. When a person's waking life is in crisis, the dream, in compensation, will adopt an affirming voice. If a person is living according to ego-centred concerns, the compensation will be subversive. To put it succinctly, dreams bring down the proud and raise the lowly (Lk 1:52).

Parables. Jesus also identified the kingdom through the narration of parables. A parable, like a dream, can surprise us with a new insight or envision the unexpected: forgiveness is offered even when it is not deserved (Lk 15:11-32) and those dubbed 'wasters' are treated with dignity (Mt 20:1-16). Like the joy of finding a lost coin (Lk 15:8-10) dreams sometimes delight us with solutions to frustrating problems. In overturning the laws of this world, Jesus was making manifest the latent power of the kingdom. Even the telling of the parable, or a dream, can itself be an in-breaking of the kingdom (Lk 4:21) and do more to deliver some insight to a person than a drawn-out analysis. Jesus' parables were distinctive in frequently being open-ended. We do not know whether or not the elder brother was reconciled with his younger sibling (Lk 15:11-32). Likewise, dreams often conclude with a dilemma rather than a happy ending. This device focuses attention on the listener or dreamer, as if to say, 'now it's over to you.'

Miracles. Jesus showed the power of God's kingdom by working miracles. The historicity of many of the nature miracles (such as calming the storm or walking on water) is doubted by biblical scholars. These testify more to Christian belief in Jesus as Lord of creation than accurately reflecting events in Jesus' ministry. On the other hand, his reputation as a healer was probably foundational to Jesus' fame and based on fact. Many of the heal-

ing miracles were linked to forgiveness (Jn 9:1-3), thereby show-
ing the power of God over the biblically related evils of sin and
sickness. Imagined miraculous feats are frequent in dreams.
Like many of the gospel miracles, these can be wonders of nature
(such as flying through the air), whereby fantastic and physically
impossible events are envisaged. Other dream-miracles concern
healing and are often more realistic: they might imagine recon-
ciliation with an enemy, or the final resolution of a protracted
problem.

Concern for the health of mind and body is a frequent theme
in dreams. In the classical world dream sanctuaries dedicated to
the Greek god of medicine, Asclepius, were used to find cures.
Classical psychotherapy essentially provides for the same end:
healing through dreamwork. As well as answering specific
health problems dreams can provide a doorway to the hidden
meaning of life. For Jung the healing significance of the dream
occurs principally in its ability to constellate archetypal symbols. By its *transcendent function* the psyche produces an archetypal symbol which heals the rift between the conscious and the
unconscious. Jung did not intend this term to be understood in a
religious sense. However, as with a gospel miracle, healing
dream symbols typically appear as a spontaneous and welcome
response to a cry for help.

Table Fellowship. Togetherness around the table was a key
sign of God's kingdom for Jesus. The promise of God's susten-
ance is made real by the acts of kindness and harmony which are
part of a shared meal. Whereas John the Baptist and the other
prophets were austere, Jesus wanted his disciples to joyfully anticipate now the heavenly banquet (Isa 25:6-9; Lk 7:33-35). He ate
with the sinner and the outcast as a sign of the unity of God's
family. These aspects of the kingdom are renewed whenever the
Eucharist is celebrated.

In dreams the strength of the ego is reduced and the relational
aspect of our identity emphasised. Dreams often envision possibilities for greater social harmony than we actually experience. I
think this aspiration was held by the seminarian who had the
following dream: 'I am in the College dining room. There are
rectangular tables: arranged with a path down the middle, and
two narrower ones from both sides. The light is dim and there is

no noise. It is suppertime.' The dreamer then notices a number of friends he has regrettably not seen for some time. The setting suggests that they have all been brought together for renewed fellowship. In reality, mealtime at the seminary refectory was noisy, hurried and sometimes tense. In the dream the atmosphere is calm and collected. The space is rearranged to form a cross. This meal setting, like the Last Supper, imagines the Christian way. Communion occurs through the remembrance of others at table in a spirit of self-sacrificial love.

Finally, a parallel can be drawn between kingdom table fellowship and the sharing of dreams. The regular sharing of dreams with your family or work colleagues can, like the Eucharist, be a powerful forum for community and anticipate the joy of being together in God's kingdom.

Spirituality

A ladder set up on the earth, reaching to heaven.
Gen 28:12

Day 22: Foundations for Spirituality

Our ancestors took the existence of God and the importance of spirituality for granted. Since the Age of the Enlightenment, a rational interaction with the material world has become the primary focus. At face value, this shift seems to have contributed more to the development of humanity than millennia of God-centredness. Today, while most still believe in God's existence, our inability to apply rational-scientific methods to spiritual experience has diminished the credibility of religious claims. As the old certainties about religion have been stripped away many either ignore God's existence or, in fewer cases, disown modernity, clinging to religion in a fundamentalist way. Even theology is dominated by rational and scientific methods. It emphasises what can be observed, such as the content of the Bible and tradition, rather than spiritual experience as such. To put it in Jungian terms, we now think in *signs* which point to something known rather than *symbols* which echo the unknown.

Contemporary consciousness is equally aware that many issues will never be resolved by scientific exploration. Spirituality today springs from such questions: Why am I here? What is the destiny of my life? A range of experiences from suffering, to encountering beauty and feeling guilty all make us aware of an unknowable yet personable divine presence.

The need for a spiritual focus becomes particularly evident at mid-life. Jung compared life to one day: sunrise until noon, followed by a gradual descent into nightfall.[1] The project of the first part is the strengthening of the ego. As infants we are still connected to our parents. Only at puberty is a person psychologically born and a sense of selfhood established. Then we go about trying to successfully make our mark in the world. But a

---

1. C. C. Jung, 'The Stages of Life' (1931) CW 8, par. 778.

Lebenswende (life turning point) typically occurs in the mid to late thirties. The one-sided focus on ego development is replaced by an adaptation to the unconscious. This can be triggered by a disappointment, an illness or a bereavement that makes us sense the futility of material goals, given our mortal nature:

> Among all my patients in the second half of life – that is to say, over thirty-five – there has not been one whose problem in the last resort was not that of finding a religious outlook on life. It is safe to say that every one of them felt ill because he had lost that which the living religions of every age have given to their followers, and none of them has been really healed who did not regain his religious outlook.[2]

Even if our ambitions for work and intimacy are met, a search for a dimension to underpin the meaning and purpose of life will be there. A failure to discern our Absolute Horizon, as Rahner called it, has serious consequences for psychological health.

Being present to ourselves and the world around us is a key disposition for cultivating a spiritual life. It is essential for developing a sense of our own identity, which in turn enables a relationship with God. In this electronic age, constantly bombarded by sound and image, the human imagination has become saturated and dulled. Our night dreams are one of the few remaining ways that we truly listen to ourselves and the movement of God's Spirit. Little wonder that those deprived of sleep become mentally disturbed. They lose one of the most important ways in which we remember who we are.

In Shakespeare's *King Lear* the monarch abdicates and gradually loses all sense of himself. During a descent into madness he asks: 'Who is it who can tell me who I am?'[3] We typically answer that question with reference to our *persona* at work or in the home, or with friends. A reflective lifestyle will also help the process of self-discovery. However, there is something that even the most profound insights and closest friends will fail to reveal. The fact that we experience ourselves as mystery points to the

2. C. G. Jung, 'Psychotherapists or the Clergy' (1932) CW 11, par. 509.
3. W. Shakespeare, *King Lear*, act 1, scene 4.238.

existence of a hidden spiritual realm and ultimately the mystery of God.

In the journey toward God we must not just know the truth about ourselves, but truly accept it. The difficulty in remembering and understanding dreams is perhaps best explained by a reluctance to truly accept ourselves. We have many reasons for self-loathing or self-rejection and invent a myriad of mechanisms for avoiding painful home truths. These range from masking self-doubt with bravura, to self-medication, to an acting out of resentment towards others that we really hold for ourselves. Dreams remind us of who we are, behind the illusions which the ego effects during the day. For the person of faith, God's unconditional love makes it possible to accept the burden of our true selves and to be ourselves before God.

On the basis of self-knowledge and self-acceptance, Lear could have answered much of his question. A relationship with God would also have helped! It was said that Jesus knew what was in a person (Jn 2:25). In our journey of personal discovery only God has the final solution. This is illustrated in the choice of Simon as the leader of the apostles (Mt 16:13-20). In this passage, not only did Simon identify Jesus as the Messiah, the Anointed one of God, but also discovered his true identity as the Rock for the community of followers. Spirituality not only leads us toward God, but to a more complete understanding of who we are meant to be.

Christian spirituality is founded on belief in a Trinitarian God. It involves acknowledging my existence as part of God's creation. Considering life as gift makes us fundamentally grateful. An attitude which does not allow for the Creator's existence makes me possessive, suspicious and resentful when forced to let go.

A Christian spirituality puts on the mind of Christ and acknowledges him as our divine brother and saviour (Phil 2:1-11). The New Testament does not report the dreams of Jesus, but the model for a spiritual life laid down by Jesus does appreciate the relevance of interior experience. Jesus emphasised the kingdom of God as happening within (Lk 17:21) rather than through the external practices of religion. In Jesus, the 'with-us-God' (Immanuel), we are brought into an intimate relationship with

God, one that connects us heart to heart with the divine. In no other monotheistic religion can we address God as Daddy ('Abba' Mk 14:36). In joining our consciousness with that of Jesus, God can be encountered through interior experience, the type at which dreaming excels.

In the Christian vision it is God who makes us holy. Spirituality is based on God's activity in us, rather than our own efforts. The popular image for a spiritual person is someone so meek and mild as to not really belong to this world. This stereotype is not authentic to Christianity, a religion founded on the incarnation of God and one which encourages engagement with rather than flight from material experience. The biblical terms for Spirit (*ruach* in Hebrew and *pneuma* in Greek), imply something additional to the material rather than in opposition to it (1 Cor 2:14-15). Natural wisdom and the Wisdom of God are often complementary, since reason is part of God's creation. However, only the influence of God's Spirit and only in faith can we truly come into contact with the divine, as God is also beyond the boundaries of nature.

Day 23: The Alchemy of Dreams

Most dreams are disagreeable, confronting us with issues we would prefer to avoid like being caught in an embarrassing situation, failing an exam or suffering the loss of a loved one. Such dreams depict the vulnerabilities we largely manage to repress by day. Fortunately, conscious life may be in better shape than our dreamscape would suggest. When we awake with the relief that 'it was only a dream' we may also learn gratitude for life's securities.

Other dreams represent our sinfulness, whether potential or real, as perpetrators of violence, sexual promiscuity, drunkenness, theft and so on. To explain such negative dreams, Freud used the concept of disguised wish fulfillment. The dream, he said, provides a safe, sleep-preserving outlet for the secret wishes we dare not act out in waking life.

Dreams of sin are not in themselves sinful. The dream is an autonomous event, a series of images over which the sleeper lacks control. Culpability, on the other hand, requires free and conscious decision making. At times we can be shocked by the actions of our dream-ego, but must remember that it is an amoral entity. As St Augustine wrote: 'I thank you Lord for not making me responsible for my dreams.'[4]

Indeed dreams which portray us as sinful may serve a moral purpose. They encourage the dreamer to look beyond surface appearances. We are neither as good nor as self-assured as we think. Such dreams typically point out the consequences of immorality. One of Jung's clients dreamt: 'I was standing in a strange garden and picked an apple from a tree. I looked about cautiously, to make sure that no one saw me.'[5] The man associated

4. Augustine, *Confession*, 10.30.
5. C. G. Jung, 'General Aspects of Dream Psychology' (1916/1948) CW 8, par. 457.

the image with the guilt he had as a child for stealing fruit from a neighbour's tree. The same feelings had occurred in relation to a clandestine affair he had recently begun with a housemaid. In the analysis of this dream Jung linked the man's remorse to the shame of Adam and Eve after their fall from grace (Gen 3:16-19). The dream served a conscience-forming function by confronting the man with his immoral behaviour.

Dreams reveal aspects of ourselves that are less proper, but nonetheless present. The interior conflict between consciously held values and the unconscious *shadow* stimulates critical self-evaluation. The shadow of a good person may feel negative and unworthy, but it is morally neutral and actually provides a more rounded self-concept than that of the *persona*. An engagement with our less worthy characteristics in the virtual reality of dreams can circumvent its projection in waking life. What we name in ourselves, we claim as being of ourselves and thereby prevent its involuntary enactment.

Even so, the conscious memory of dreams can lead to personal failure by promoting immoral images. Christian tradition teaches that in dreams we are sensitive to the voice of evil as well as good. It was for this reason that classical theologians advocated prayerful preparation for sleep. St Thomas counselled the avoidance of meat for supper and the careful practice of chastity prior to bedtime so that the mind would not be unduly contaminated prior to sleep![6]

Christian dream analysis is best conducted in a spirit of discernment so that only signs of God's ways are embraced. Since medieval times, the church has developed a set of criteria for judging the validity of a private revelation. These might also be used when evaluating the religious implications of a dream. Firstly, the message is acceptable only when it is consistent with the gospel. Secondly, personal holiness increases the capacity of the person to have a valid spiritual experience. Religiously oriented people are more likely to have spiritually influenced dreams. However, St Thomas maintained that divine revelation can also be independent of the recipient's holiness given that it is intended for the general good.[7] Thus the pagan king

6. T. Aquinas, *Summa Theologica*, II Q.154 Art.5.
7. T. Aquinas, *Summa Theologica*, II-II Q.172 Art.4.

Nebuchadnezzar had a divinely inspired dream (Dan 4:1-18) and Saul, while a persecutor of Christians, had a vision of the risen Christ (Acts 9:1-19). The third criterion concerns the fruits of the experience. A spiritual event which leads to prayer, conversion and good works is more likely to be authentic. To be genuine, a religious dream should witness to the fruits of the Spirit: love, joy, peace, patience, kindness, goodness, trustfulness, gentleness and self-control (Gal 5:22-23).

Jung likewise held that the dream message should be tested against conscious standards of behaviour. However, he liked the dream's amoral and uncensored quality. He compared dreams to the *vas bene clausum* (well sealed vessel) with which the medieval alchemists worked. Using this apparatus, alchemy attempted the transformation of base metals such as lead into priceless gold. In a similar way, the psyche attempts to effect maturity out of the *prima materia* (base material) of the unconscious within the privileged enclosure of the dream.

Modelled on alchemy, Jung argued that Christianity should engage with the base elements of human nature in its striving for the 'gold' of spiritual transformation:

> We should not rise above the earth with the aid of spiritual intuitions and run away from hard realities. ... That we are bound to the earth does not mean that we cannot grow; on the contrary it is the *sine qua non* of growth. No noble, well-grown tree ever disowned its dark roots, for it grows not only upward but downward as well.[8]

Where religion promotes contact with the unconscious it contributes to psychological health. A spirituality which is too sweet is not wholesome. However, there is an important distinction between *knowing* the darkness of your life, and *incorporating* it into your personality. While Christianity accepts the spiritual wisdom of acknowledging one's vulnerabilities, it attaches no intrinsic value to evil. The Christian faith seeks transformation primarily through transcendence. Holiness is not 'wholeness' but (as the Hebrew word '*qdsh*' implies) a 'separation' from all that is base (Isa 6:3).

Jung understood the incidence of animals in dreams as repre-

---

8. C. G. Jung, *Psychology and Alchemy* (1935/1953) CW 12, par. 148.

senting the base and instinctual elements of the personality. The religious dimensions of these images are demonstrated by animal images for God in the Bible such as the eagle (Deut 32:11), the dove (Mk 1:10) and the lamb (Jn 1:29). Over decades of dream analysis, Jung found much evidence for interpreting animal dream imagery as highlighting the need to integrate the instinctual.

Take the example of the snake, a frequent animal image in dreams. For Freud it was an important symbol for the penis. Jung, by contrast, interpreted it as an expression of the unconscious since that central, yet hidden, part of the human anatomy, the spine, has a serpentine form. In dreams the image of a snake might well evoke fear and represent the threat posed by the unconscious. However, the snake also has a beguiling aspect. This frightening yet appealing effect finds notable corroboration in the incident from the Book of Numbers where poisonous serpents were sent by God to punish the people for their loss of patience during the Exodus (Num 21: 4-9; Jn 3:14-15). The snake attack ultimately brought about the people's conversion. Moses then fashioned a bronze serpent, which, when gazed upon, acted as an antidote to the poison. A mortal danger paradoxically became a source of salvation. Similarly, even though the 'bite' of the unconscious threatens, it can also be a source of healing and new life.

Day 24: Incubation

People sometimes wake up with the solution to a problem that has been 'slept on'. This experience can vary from a general sense of encouragement to a specific direction suggested by the imagery of the dream. In a famous example, Friedrich A. Kekulé von Stradonitz (1829-1896) dreamt of a snake biting its tail. The German chemist had been researching the formula for benzene and had fallen asleep in his chair. This dream elucidated the structure of that molecule as hexagonal rather than linear. The insight revolutionised organic chemistry.

Attributing the problem solving capacity of dreams to the supernatural, ancient religions developed the practice of *incubation*. The god would visit a person during sleep to provide inspiration, healing and guidance. In classical Greece the cult of Asclepius, a god of healing, involved dream incubation. At its height there were three hundred Asclepia including the temples at Epidauros, Pergamon, Kos and Athens. Four parts were observed in the ritual:

1. The ill person would travel to the dream sanctuary following the advice of a dream. The Asclepion was scenically located and had an extensive sacred precinct.
2. On arrival, temple attendants ascertained the pilgrim's needs and a ritual purification followed. This included fasting and drinking water from sacred fountains.
3. The patient would sleep that night in an underground chamber, the *abaton*. The walls of this room would be inscribed with the testimonies of previous miracles. Asclepius would appear in a dream or vision and perform a symbolic operation on the ailment. Alternatively the god would issue a prescription of treatment. In other cases the healing or prescription were transmitted in a less explicit dream.
4. The person would awaken already cured or the prescription

contained in the dream would be administered by a temple attendant. In the former case it is notable that the dream itself, and not the subsequent interpretation, was seen to have therapeutic effect. This corresponds to the automatic ability of dreams to bestow healing, even in the absence of recollection and analysis.

Though dream sanctuaries were prohibited by Judaism, the dream of Jacob's ladder (Gen 28:10-22) follows the structure of an incubation ritual: a journey undertaken at a time of crisis to the place of dreaming, preparation, a dream in which God is made known and the dreamer's response. The centrepiece of the dream is a ladder on which Jacob saw angels moving and hearing the voice of God promising him land, descendants and protection. The Hebrew term for 'ladder' (*sulam*), occurring uniquely here, is reminiscent of Mesopotamian temple towers (ziggurats) which had such a stairway. This led to a summit where the deity would communicate with mortals. The ramp represented a bridge between heaven and earth.

Jacob described the ladder as the 'gate to heaven' (Gen 28:17). The stone which he used for a pillow was then set up as a monument to the experience (Gen 28:18). It resembles the sacred pillars of Canaanite worship. These were condemned in the Bible (Deut 7:5; Hos 10:1-2; Mic 5:13) in an effort to preserve the purity of Judaism. The strength of the condemnation suggests that some Jews actually engaged in these esoteric forms of spirituality.

The dream of Solomon at the sanctuary of Gibeon even more clearly meets the criteria for a ritual incubation (1 Kings 3:4-15; 2 Chr 1:6-12). Solomon went to Gibeon to receive a dream oracle. He offered sacrifice and lay down to sleep. The Lord appeared in a dream and conversed with him. God granted Solomon's request for a wise and understanding heart. Afterwards, albeit in Jerusalem, Solomon responded to the dream revelation with a festival of thanksgiving. The later parallel version of this incident in the Book of Chronicles describes Solomon's experience as a vision rather than a dream. This was with respect to a more critical view of spiritual dreamwork as Judaism developed.

Incubation has continued to be a latent feature in religious tradition. As we on read on Day 17, some of the dream narratives in the *Confession* of St Patrick are introduced with the phrase *'responsum divinum'*. This suggests that Patrick considered dreams as a 'divine response' to his problems. We can imagine that having prayed over his situation Patrick would have gone to sleep in the hope of receiving a communication from God in the dreams of that night. His earnest cry for help was sometimes met with a divinely inspired solution.

The same notion of informal incubation is evident in the Jewish ritual of *she'elat chalom*, whereby the Lord is asked to answer a problem with a dream.[9] A written question is placed under the pillow and the person decides to be receptive to a divinely gifted dream that night.

The reserve of the Judeo-Christian tradition on the practice of incubation is due to our sense of the transcendence and freedom of God. Incubation might be interpreted as a human attempt to control the spiritual. In particular the use of incubation risks the practice of oneiromancy, a form of divination whereby a person tries to uncover God's will through dream analysis. This is condemned in the Bible (Deut 13:2-6; Zech 10:2) and Christian tradition. Insight into the future is regarded as a gift from God, not a human entitlement. It is for the same reason that the church disapproves the reading of tarot cards, the use of Ouija boards, and astrology. These are human efforts to possess an intelligence that belongs, by right, to God alone.

Mindful of this reserve, some of the principles of dream incubation might well be adapted for use today. The aim here is to allow the wisdom of God to work with our own wisdom as we engage in dreamwork from a spiritual viewpoint. Firstly we should spend some time in prayerful recollection in the hours before sleep, commending a notable issue to God. The placing of a religious symbol in the bedroom will reinforce the spiritual dimensions of the exercise. Speaking to a confidant will also strengthen the motivation for finding a new perspective and reduce the strength of resistance to a solution from a dream. You might well briefly write out the nature of the problem, formulating the question about which you seek guidance and place this piece of paper under your pillow.

9. J. Covitz, *Visions of the Night. A Study of Jewish Dream Interpretation* (Boston: Shambala, 1990), 133-134.

After the night's sleep follow the usual routine for dream retrieval. Include a prayer of thanks to God for any remembered dream. Finally narrate the dream to your mentor or record it in your journal. Each dream element is discussed and the possible interpretations are identified. The benefit of this exercise ranges from a focusing on our situation before God, to the reception of a divinely inspired dream solution.

Day 25: Using Dream Images in Prayer

Not all experience is of equal merit. Striking images, including those from dreams, express our faith in ways more redolent than words. They call for prayerful reflection and discernment. Even the apparently most trivial perception can potentially carry a spiritual significance. But we must develop an openness to receive these seeds of God's presence:

> Every moment and every event of every man's life on earth plants something in his soul. For just as the wind carries thousands of winged seeds, so each moment brings with it germs of spiritual vitality that come to rest imperceptibly in the minds and wills of men. Most of these unnumbered seeds perish and are lost, because men are not prepared to receive them: for such seeds as these cannot spring up anywhere except in the good soil of freedom, spontaneity and love.[10]

Religious images, including those from dreams, are distinguished by a number of factors. They are numinous, expressing the wonder and awe of being in God's presence. They are symbolic pointing to something 'more' than their appearance. They often imagine healing, anticipating, if only for a moment, the hope for salvation. Religious images also challenge us to walk in God's ways, reminding us how to live our faith with others.

Jung developed the technique of *active imagination* as a way of exploring significant dream images. Unlike dreaming, active imagination is a process over which we have a measure of control. It is an intentional act that occurs while the conscious is active. However, as with dreaming, the technique evokes the unconscious by using the *imagination*. The critical faculties of consciousness are weakened so that unconscious processes are

10. T. Merton, *New Seeds of Contemplation* (New York: New Directions, 1961), 15.

engaged. Active imagination is essentially a conversation between the conscious ego and a product of the unconscious. The
process is generally elaborated in four steps by Jungian analysts.
A similar pattern might be used when we encounter an image
with religious dimensions.

1. You choose an image or figure from a selected dream.
   Welcome the image into awareness. You then concentrate on
   that object with eyes closed in a place that is free of distraction. In this meditative state, the image becomes animated
   and takes on a life of its own. You remain disposed to the
   movement.

2. In the second stage, your ego engages with the activated
   image. A dialogue is conducted with the figures drawn from
   the imagination. Focus on the important feelings evoked by
   the image. Remember that in most cases the dream represents
   aspects of the dreamer. In other words, at this stage a part of
   our own unconscious is being experienced and better understood.

3. Thirdly, the result of the fantasy is given external form in
   painting, writing, modelling or enactment through dance.
   This should be done with as little interference as possible
   from the conscious, so that the unconscious is still allowed to
   speak for itself. The product of the unconscious then becomes the basis for a further reflection, through an exploration of parallels in literature and mythology. In the context
   of a religious image an associated passage of scripture can be
   studied and prayed over. The dream journal is a good forum
   for this work.

4. Fourthly, the practical implications of the product are elicited.
   See what the image is calling you to do. These conclusions
   are measured against ethical standards and confirmed by the
   analyst or spiritual director. In this way the process goes beyond personal meditation and the public implications of the
   dream image are established.

Jung's method of active imagination has a significant preced-
ent in Christian tradition. It resembles the technique of meditation used by St Ignatius of Loyola (1491-1566) in the *Spiritual
Exercises*. Here also interior images are visualised and a dialogue

is initiated between the ego and the image. Ignatius based his meditations on passages from the Bible or theological reflections on, for example, creation, the incarnation and hell. In each of the spiritual exercises there is a calling to mind of the grace needed, meditation on a particular image and a colloquy or intimate conversation with Christ.

For Ignatius, the salvific power of God comes alive in the person who meditates on sacred images. Specifically, the practice helps an individual to find and embrace the will of God. The chosen material is best illuminated by God in the person who achieves complete openness or 'indifference' before God. Ignatius noted two principal feeling-based spiritual movements in the exercises: *consolation*, which generally leads toward God and *desolation* which is usually the work of the Adversary. However for the unconverted, the devil consoles, while God challenges.

Take the example of the gospel story of the Widow of Nain (Lk 7:11-17). Having read the passage, the meditator pictures the scene, paying particular attention to any emotions it evokes. You may feel consoled by the solidarity of those gathered with the widow and desolate in our inability to remedy suffering and death. Focusing on Jesus' sympathy for the widow helps us appreciate his solidarity with the human condition. His power to bring new life from death is the foundation of our hope. The grace available in this passage might be a share in the compassion of Jesus and a strengthening of our own abilities to lead people to new life.

Exploring a dream so as to gain insight into its meaning is one thing, acting on that message is the necessary final step in the process. Spiritual dreamwork furthers the willingness to follow God's call in our conscious lives. Dreams are normally a response by the unconscious to the dreamer's conscious situation and may well invite some practical course of action.

For Robert Johnson the lessons acquired from dreamwork are really learnt when they are ritualised. In one example, a man dreamt of consuming huge amounts of junk food only to remain emaciated.[11] The dream analysis indicated that his lifestyle was

11. R. Johnson, *Inner Work. Using Dreams and Active Imagination for Personal Growth* (San Francisco: Harper and Row, 1986), 97-99.

not providing nourishment. The dreamer ritualised this interpretation by purchasing a meal at a McDonald's restaurant and
solemnly burying it in his garden. He thus reinforced the decision to abandon self-starving behaviours through a symbolic action. Just as Jacob set up a stone monument to the dream of the
ladder (Gen 28:18), so we might consider some reminder of the
insight gained from a dream.

Day 26: Dreamwork in Spiritual Direction

The most important examples of dream analysis in Hebrew scripture were conducted in public settings and the interpretation was viewed as having social effects (Gen 20, 41; Dan 2, 4). By contrast, dreamwork has largely been professionalised and privatised in modern times. However, a retrieval of dreamwork in everyday and communal settings is now underway. This is clearly the case with contemporary dreamgroups, such as the type proposed in this book.

A regard for the social importance of dreams is a feature of traditional society. Kilton Stewart's landmark anthropological study of the Senoi of Malaysia in 1934, described a society with remarkably little crime and high standards of mental health. He attributed this to their use of dreams:

> Breakfast in the Senoi house is like a dream clinic, with the father and older brothers listening to and analysing the dreams of all the children. At the end of the family clinic the male population gathers in the council, at which the dreams of the family council and all the men in the community are reported, discussed and analysed.[12]

When an acquaintance figured in a dream, the dreamer examined the relevant waking relationship. Where the dream indicated hostility to others in the community, possible corrections would be discussed among the group involving both the dreamer and the characters represented. The dream might also be given expression in a poem, a song or artwork. All of this purged the conflict represented by the dream and prevented social tension in the community.

In Western society today, a renewal of the social dimension

---

12. K. Stewart, 'Dream Theory in Malaya' in C. T. Tart (ed), *Altered States of Consciousness* (New York: John Wiley and Sons, 1969), 164.

of dreamwork could begin in the home, with a regular family dream meeting similar to that of the Senoi. This might simply be a breakfast-time invitation to share dreams from the night before. The telling of dreams will make for a more profound family conversation and complement conscious plans for the day with the point that we are more than our activities. The exercise will also promote ongoing dream recall. It is likely that those sleeping under the same roof will have dreams about each other.

Discussing your dreams with a spiritual director is another possibility for giving dreamwork an interpersonal dimension. An axiom of Christian spirituality direction states that we are not good judges of our own case ('*nemo judex in causa sua*'). A spiritual mentor provides an invaluable forum for personal accountability and discernment of God's will. In the Celtic church a person without an *anamchara* (soul-friend) was likened to a body without a head. Today the ministry of spiritual direction is enjoying a renaissance within the church.

Soul-friendship is like ordinary friendship in being warm and life-enhancing. It is dissimilar to friendship in that inner thoughts and reactions are more the subject matter of the conversation than the public life of the directee. Soul-friendship is normally conceived as a one-way relationship. The soul-friend keeps the distance necessary to maintain objectivity and allow the person to speak honestly, knowing that the director's own needs are not at stake. Honesty is facilitated by a non-judgemental attitude on the part of the director and a pledge to maintain confidentiality. The soul-friend is given access to a holy place and must tread softly.

The soul-friend's role is largely facilitative, creating a safe environment and then waiting patiently for the presence of God to be noticed in the experience of the befriended. Jungians likewise describe the relationship between analyst and client as circumscribed by a *tenemos*. This term refers to the classical Greek custom of designating the boundaries of a temple with a furrow. It describes the privilege that surrounds the analysis and allows the client to speak about personal issues in a safe way.

Soul friendship should have agreed aims, an established frequency of meetings and a periodic review of the relationship. The spiritual mentor cultivates an intimacy with the befriended yet preserves the freedom of the person to be themselves. He or she is an educator in the truest sense of the word. The word 'education' is based on the Latin verb '*educare*', which implies that teaching is a 'leading out' of something that is already within. The goal of spiritual mentoring is the discovery of one's inner purpose and vocation from God. This is 'led out' through the dialogue with the soul-friend.

Dreams are a fertile ground for the conversation with a soul friend. The dream's capacity for accurate self-reflection is taken a step further when it is told to another. Dream language has a capacity to summarise personal embarrassments in a subtle way. Sharing a relevant dream is often a good method for introducing a particular issue. Dreams also point to the strength of our emotions. These are an often repressed component of the personality and dreamwork makes for their safe expression. The honesty which is important in soul-friendship is not merely the intellectual recognition of personal facts, but allows for the release of associated emotions. This catharsis itself has a powerful effect.

Dreams not only diagnose the psychological situation but also suggest compensations and guidance. The person who uses dreams in soul-friendship learns to confront personal complexes and accepts the advice for personal growth provided by the archetypes. The spiritual mentor has a role in identifying possible ways in which the higher wisdom of God's Spirit is speaking through a person's dreams.

The spiritual director's approach to the dream should be both passive and active. A passive stance is based on a recognition that the dream exists in relation to the dreamer. The soul-friend should resist the temptation to explain the dream or offer intuitive hunches as to its meaning. Only the dreamer can interpret the dream. However, the mentor's role in the dream analysis also has an active aspect. To amplify a particular dream image, he or she may suggest a text in scripture that can be associated with the dream. This would help interpret the dreamer's situation in light of the Word of God. The director's knowledge of the nature and function of dreams can provide a helpful introduction to the person who wishes to bring dreams to the soul-friendship.

Dreamwork in spiritual direction should be limited. Dream analysis should not dominate the encounter since soul-friendship is primarily concerned with the life of prayer and lived faith. It does not seek to probe the depths of the unconscious, nor can it resolve the issues which might bring a person to professional psychotherapy. Dreamwork should be regarded as being one element rather than an essential aspect of the relationship.

Soul-friendship is best provided by those with a level of personal holiness, knowledge of the Bible and Christian tradition and an ability to abide by the boundaries of the relationship. Indeed the role has normally been regarded as a formal ministry within the church. However, it can also happen in less formal ways. When two people realise that, in their conversation, God is being encountered, that dialogue too fulfils the key aim of spiritual direction.

Day 27: The Darkest Night

Every so often we have a sleepless and deeply troubled night, when our fears plague us and all sense of security is absent. St John of the Cross used his experience of the *noche oscura* (dark night) to describe growth in holiness. He defined two types of spiritual night.

In the *night of the senses*, all feelings of consolation are withdrawn and we realise how alone we are in the world. This is actually a time of grace. An infant must at some stage be weaned off its mother if it is to grow up. Giving up the dependency of infancy allows for a genuine two-way relationship to develop between parent and child. In the same way, as we face up to our responsibilities, we grow in maturity. Or we may, at this time, be tempted into a perpetual state of childish self-indulgence.

In the second night, the *night of the soul*, John of the Cross says that we lose even that consolation that comes from personal responsibility. We sense the futility of life, despite our best efforts. We painfully realise that life ends with decline and death. John of the Cross describes the pain of this night as a complete sense of God's absence. Like the crucified Jesus, we experience a deep loneliness: 'My God, my God, why have you forsaken me?' (Mk 15:34) This terrifying insight too can ultimately be a time of grace. It frees us from the obligation to be masters of our own destiny and allows us to hand over our life to God without conditions. For those who simply endure with pure faith, the dark night will eventually give way to a bright dawn.

It is our ability to hope, even when there is no reason to do so, that creates dreams of a better future. Along with faith and love, Christianity regards hope as a theological virtue, one which has its origin and goal in God (1 Cor 13:13). Hope is linked to faith in being based on trust in God's care. The existence of God underpins our hopes. It can also be linked to our imitation of the God who is love (1 Jn 4:8). Hopes are realised through our loving. People who love give others reason to hope. In short, our hope is based on faith in God and is found wherever love is expressed.

The whole thrust of the Old Testament is the hope that God's promises would be fulfilled, notwithstanding reasons to despair. At the foundation of Israel, the elderly couple Abraham and Sarah trusted in God and then they were gifted with a son, something humanly impossible (Gen 17:15-19). In Egypt the people hoped that God would lead them into a promised land of milk and honey (Ex 3:17). Centuries later, even as Israel was being destroyed as a political entity, the prophets dreamt of a newly constituted People of God (Jer 30:3). It was in the context of captivity in Babylon that Isaiah created a remarkable vision of an idyllic world (Isa 65:17-25). The darker their situation became, the more radical became the nation's hope. When all was lost, the biblical authors resorted to an apocalyptic vision, the wish for a dramatic intervention by God on behalf of his people (Ezek 37:1-14).

The New Testament presents Jesus as the fulfillment of the people's hopes. Death, the ultimate cause for despair, has been defeated by his resurrection (1 Cor 15). Believers are joined to this pledge of eternal life by the sacrament of baptism. In the early church, the link between baptism and the resurrection was clear in that it was conducted at night during the Easter Vigil. The baptised person lit a candle from the paschal fire to celebrate the light of new life shining through the darkness of sin and death.

Our dreams can also address the hope of life after death. For example, a man who had become depressed by his terminal illness had a dream which replayed significant scenes from his life.[13] The conclusion of the dream pictured the man lying on his deathbed. A doctor announced 'he's gone' and a clock on the mantlepiece stopped. Then a window opened and a bright light appeared. He walked out on the brilliant path and disappeared. Though time had stopped he had gone into a timeless realm. Following the dream the man felt deep contentment. Similarly, a

---

13. J. Sanford, *Dreams. God's Forgotten Language* (New York: J. B. Lippincott, 1968), 59-60.

hospice patient who had been a ship's captain dreamt of setting out on an exciting sea voyage over uncharted waters.[14] The dream transformed his fear of death into a sense of adventure and expectation.

Jung recorded the dreams a ten year old girl, as told to her father shortly before death.[15] Neither was Christian and she was not aware of the concept of resurrection, yet she experienced many dream images of new life during her final illness. In the first dream a monster devours many animals, but then they are reborn. In the eleventh dream the girl is dangerously ill. Suddenly birds come out of her skin and cover her completely. For Jung, this case showed that the concept of eternal life has an archetypal basis that is independent of consciously learnt beliefs.

Dreams concerning death are generally interpreted as the termination of an aspect of the personality and the birth of something new. The old position must 'die' to enable the creation of a new identity. Such dreams usually occur at times of transition from one stage in life to the next. In some cases, however, dreams prepare the person for physical death or reflect on that event in the aftermath of bereavement. The experience of a dearly departed one appearing in a dream about one year after death is not uncommon. Jung dreamt of his parents following their deaths in this manner. Such dreams witness to our innate hope in life beyond mortal existence and provide reassurance to the bereaved. In these dreams the deceased person is typically at peace and appears to be in the prime of life once again.

Dreams of finding new life do not underestimate the difficulty of making the transition from this life to the next. Authentic hope is grounded in a realistic sense of life's challenges and a willingness to confront them. This is apparent in the case of a retired woman who took part in one of my dreamgroups. She shared a dream of being captive in a desert among a group of forty. A narrow path leading up a steep mountain provides an

---

14. P. Bulkley, 'Invitation at the Threshold. Pre-Death Spiritual Experiences' in K. Bulkeley (ed), *Among All these Dreamers* (Albany, NY: SUNY, 1996), 157-159.
15. C. G. Jung, 'Symbols and the Interpretation of Dreams' (1961) CW 18, pars. 525-535.

escape route, but the prisoners must sneak off individually and discreetly. Then the escape attempt came to the attention of the captors and the people break for freedom in a panic stricken way. But she is infirm and unable to keep up. Three elderly gentlemen come up behind her. They excuse themselves as they clamber over her and nimbly make their way up the mountain. She gives up. Then two hands appear out of the sky. They lift her to the top of the mountain, where all her needs for food, security and friendship are provided, even without asking.

The resolution of this dream resembles Isaiah's depiction of new life in his vision of a heavenly banquet (Isa 25:6-9). The woman's dream affirms that when all seems lost new life comes from God. When we are unable to save ourselves and when no-one else will help, God will lend a helping hand.

Day 28: 'What is Your Myth?'

Dreaming is our personal storytelling time. By telling our pre-occupations to ourselves, much as we would to a friend, dreams discharge anxiety and provide a sense of who we are. Both the fear of falling asleep and the difficulty in recalling dreams might well be linked to a reluctance to face the reality check we receive every night in our dreams.

It was originally the Greek philosopher Aristotle (384-322) who attributed dreams to a paradoxical sensitivity in sleep.[16] While the sleeping body seems less responsive, it is actually finely attuned to stimuli. Dreams can incorporate noises from the sleeping environment or indicate the physical condition of the body. A dream can also be a delayed response to an event experienced in waking life but not consciously noted. Dreams can furthermore be caused by the assertion of neglected needs. With their heightened sensitivity, dreams may even transcend the boundaries of time and space, picking up minute signals of future events. Jungian psychology argues that among the stimuli which achieve awareness through dreams are the archetypes, including that of God's indwelling presence. From ridiculous trivia to sublime insight into the meaning of our lives, dreaming is an amazing aspect of human experience.

There are two ways in which a dream can be considered spiritual. Firstly, through its promotion of self-knowledge, dreamwork contributes to the integrity of a person before God. We tend to relate to God through the image of ourselves as perceived by others. Dreamwork enlarges our sense of personal identity. It allows us to see and experience our emotions in ways often denied in waking life. Dreams can propose compensations to the deficiencies present in conscious life. They also outline

---

16. Aristotle, *Parva naturalia: On Dreams*, 462a30.

aspects of our potential through a prospective function. The better we know ourselves, past, present and future, the more completely we can relate to God.

Secondly, dreams can be religious by making us aware of God's activity. The voice of God is 'a sound of sheer silence' (1 Kings 19:12) and the relaxed state of the ego during sleep enables it to be heard. The presence of God's Spirit can act as our conscience, independently asserting the distinction between right and wrong. The image of God can be represented as the ground of creation's existence. This aspect underlines God's absolute fidelity to creation and reminds us that life occurs *sub specie aeternitatis* (under the gaze of eternity). The divine presence can also be manifest in dreams through a symbol, graciously embodying aspects of the invisible God.

Christian spirituality speaks of each person being gifted by a personal relationship with God or a *personal vocation*.[17] Each of us is 'called by name' (Is 43:1) and given an unrepeatable identity before the Creator. The discovery of our personal vocation helps explain the mystery of life in its joys and sorrows. It provides a sense of coherence and direction through it all. The personal vocation positively affirms God's pledge of love. It also calls us to a life less ordinary. While our personal vocation is present from the time spent in our mother's womb (Ps 139:13), its definition is elusive. After much sifting, something of it might be expressed in a motto, an image or a story. This will seem banal to everyone except the person to whom it is addressed. The naming or imaging of one's grounding truth is an important moment in the faith journey. Spiritual mentors recommend prayer with the Bible as a means of identifying it through finding a personally resonant passage from scripture.

From the Old Testament, Noah's personal vocation might well have been represented by the rainbow. In the story of the Flood, God's retribution for humanity's evil was followed by the pledge of a new covenant. After the land dried up, God said to Noah: 'This is the sign of the covenant that I make between me and you and every living creature that is with you, for all future generations: I have set my bow in the clouds and it shall be a sign of the covenant between me and the earth.' (Gen 9:12-13) The

---

17. H. Alphonso, *The Personal Vocation* (Roma: Pomel, 1996).

rainbow symbolises the connection between heaven and earth, being rooted in natural elements, yet reaching for the sky. It combines rain and light to produce an array of colours. Life also achieves its colour in the combination of tears and brightness. This symbol explains that out of life's tear-drops, God's light makes something beautiful.

From the New Testament, the cross became a defining personal symbol for many Christians. It represents integrity in being made up of four opposing points that are held together as one. Christian spirituality combines a vertical or God-centred focus with a respect for the horizontal or social implications of holiness. It symbolises the painful interaction of opposites such as goodness and sin, life and death, heaven and hell. For Jung, the cross somehow reconciles these tensions in its quarternitarian form and finally yields a rebirth or resurrection. It thus epitomises the gospel paradox, that through self-sacrifice comes new life (Mt 10:38-39).

The equivalent concept to personal vocation in Jungian psychology is that of the personal *myth*. Jung made his life task the discovery of the eternal still-point by which an individual's life can make sense. Of himself and others he would ask: 'What is your myth?'[18] Like the individual vocation, a personal myth engages the imagination in an enchanting way. It is a far more resonant description of that central personal truth than a scientific analysis. It includes an element of the mystery which motivates as well as fulfils the search for purpose in life. As we saw on Day 12, Jung's personal myth was imaged by the mandala, a symbol for the Self.

Many people follow less than adequate myths. Psychology broadly defines the male will to power, and the female desire for intimacy as the two drives which, when followed exclusively, define many false personal vocations.[19] These impulses generate countless stories of men isolated by their ambition and women over-identified by their relationships. For psychology the truth may lie somewhere between the myths of power and love. If we

18. C. G. Jung, *Memories, Dreams, Reflections* (New York: Random House, 1963), 3, 171, 199.
19. R. May, *Love and Will* (New York: W. W. Norton, 1969).

strive to make a contribution to our world in a way that respects others, then we will achieve happiness. However, the Judeo-Christian tradition offers a different perspective, stressing the twin factors of love for God and one's neighbour as the key to fulfillment (Mt 22:39-40).

Waking life typically immerses us in functions and roles, which can diminish our sense of personal relationship with God. On the other hand, dreams serve to recollect our identity and can bestow an awareness of our innate relationship with the divine. In dreamwork we have a tool for exploring the mystery that is life, one which may even provide some inkling of our personal vocation or myth.

Appendix A:
Questions and Activities for Reflection

Week One

Day 1: Review your pattern of sleep hygiene. How can you better prepare for sleep?

Day 2: Can you observe any of the scientific findings on sleep in yourself or others?

Day 3: Recall personal experiences of the mentioned sleep conditions.

Day 4: Are dreams simply the by-product of sleep, or inherently meaningful?

Day 5: Draw up a check-list of actions that will improve your ability to retrieve dreams.

Day 6: Write out a recent dream according to the suggested narrative structure.

Day 7: Do you view sleep as a positive or negative part of your life?

Week Two

Day 8: Write about a key insight from your reading of Freud's oneirology.

Day 9: Write about a key insight from your reading of Jung's psychology.

Day 10: From your personal experience give examples of the four types of dreams.

Day 11: What neglected needs in your waking life do your dreams compensate?

Day 12: Identify a simile, metaphor, pun or symbol from your own dreams.

Day 13: Identify the appearance of the *persona, shadow, anima/animus* or the *Self* in your dreams.

Day 14: Using an image from a recent dream, list some associations and amplifications.

Week Three

Day 15: Read and reflect on these passages from the Bible:
Sir 34:1-8; Job 33:14-18.

Day 16: Read and reflect on the infancy narrative in the gospel
of Matthew: Mt 1:18-2:23.

Day 17: To what extent do dreams represent God's presence
and guidance in your life?

Day 18: Summarise the key points of Christian tradition on the
spirituality of dreams.

Day 19: Write about some aspects of your life which make you
more disposed to God.

Day 20: Describe an experience of *mysterium tremendum et
fascinans* in your life.

Day 21: Give images from your dreams which have been signs
of God's kingdom.

Week Four

Day 22: Think about some of the blocks to greater self-
knowledge and self-acceptance in your life.

Day 23: Describe a difficult experience in your life that resulted
in spiritual gold.

Day 24: Write out a current problem, place the text under your
pillow and 'sleep on it'.

Day 25: Depict a significant image from your dreams.

Day 26: Reflect on the role (existing or desired) of a soul-friend
in your life.

Day 27: Can you recall a dream which testifies to Christian
belief in the resurrection?

Day 28: Have your dreams provided any image for your
personal vocation?

Appendix B: Prayer Before and After Sleep[1]

Before Sleep:
Father in heaven,
I thank you that waking or sleeping
you are the God of my salvation.
I give to you my sleep of this night:
send dreams that will make me attentive to my life
and inspire me with insights into your kingdom.
Even in sleep let my spirit sing to you.
May your holy angels keep me in peace,
and may your blessing be always upon me.
Through Christ our Lord. Amen.

After Sleep:
Praise the Lord who has protected me this night
and gifted me with a new day.

Lord, you speak through the marvels of creation:
Open my eyes to recognise in last night's dreams
the trace of your steps.
May the memory of my dreams bless me
with understanding and new insight,
so that I may know your love
and your guiding promise.

Let your vision for creation
dawn in our world today.
Protect the weak and needy.
Heal the broken hearted.
Give bread to the hungry.
Give freedom to the oppressed.

Today, I pledge to be part of the dream,
that is your kingdom.
Through Christ our Lord. Amen.

---

1. The night prayer is adapted from R. Parker, *Healing Dreams. Their Power and Purpose in Your Spiritual Life* (London: SPCK, 1988), 24. The morning prayer is based on the language used in, L. Deiss, *Biblical Prayers* (Cincinnati, OH: World Library, 1976), 156-181.

Appendix C: Group Dreamwork

A method for group dreamwork in a non-professional setting has been developed by Montague Ullman.[2] It is presented here in a modified form. The two conditions which determine a successful dreamgroup are safety and discovery. By the safety factor, the dream presenter's privacy is upheld. All proceedings are confidential to the group. The entire process is underpinned by the voluntary nature of the self-disclosure and the non-intrusive character of questions put to the dreamer. On the other hand, the discovery factor refers to the need for the dream presenter to share the dream in order to achieve its interpretation. The volunteer attempts to offer a clear dream narrative and participates in the group discussion.

There are four parts to the analysis of a dream according to this method:

1. *Stage One: Narration* (5 minutes). The group sits in a circle and a volunteer narrates a dream. Written copies of the dream may be distributed to those present. The narrative itself should be free of interpretative comment. It should be a dream of recent origin so that the presenter can better recall its emotional residues and conscious context. Having listened to the dream-story, the group may ask questions to clarify its general sense. This stage focuses on the manifest dream. No associations with the dream or explanations of its meaning are offered by the dreamer or the dreamgroup.

2. *Stage Two: Dreamwork* (15 minutes). The dreamgroup makes the dream its own. The group adopts a meditative posture and state of mind. The dream is slowly re-read by the presenter. He or she then turns away from the other members of the group and listens to the subsequent discussion. In the first place, the others report their feelings in relation to any striking dream images. This part identifies the key points of psychic energy in the dream. Secondly, the meaning of the dream's imagery is explored. Members suggest their opinion

---

2. M. Ullman, 'The Experiential Dream Group' in M. Ullman and C. Limmer (eds), *The Variety of Dream Experience. Expanding Our Ways of Working with Dreams* (New York: Continuum, 1987), 1-26.

as to the matter represented by the various dream images. The associations offered by the group are subjective projections of each contributor and do not directly refer to the dream presenter. Thus each remark of Stage Two might well be prefaced with: 'In my dream I feel...' or 'In my dream x represents ...' The dreamer's awareness of the subjective nature of the associations offered by the group augments the safety factor in the process. At the same time members' associations contribute to the discovery factor by evoking parallels with the dreamer's situation. The transpersonal dimension of the individual is foundational to this common ground among those present.

3. *Stage Three: The Dreamer's Response* (10 minutes). The dream is returned to the dreamer, who then validates the members' contributions. The group listens to the presenter's response without interruption. Further dialogue between the dreamer and the group might clarify the circumstances in which the dream took place, both the immediate day-residue and the general life-context of the dreamer. Finally, the leader summarises the dreamwork. A judgement on the various dream images can be offered, subject to an awareness that interpretation belongs to the dreamer.

4. *Stage Four: Afterthoughts* (5 minutes). At the subsequent meeting of the dreamgroup, the dreamer reviews his or her reflections on the dream in the light of the previous group discussion. This gives the presenter an opportunity to offer some considered thoughts on the meaning of the dream.

Annotated Select Bibliography

Bulkeley, K., *The Wilderness of Dreams. Exploring the Religious Meaning of Dreams in Modern Western Culture*, Albany, NY: State University of New York Press, 1994.
An interfaith examination of the spiritual dimension in dreams.

Carskadon, M. (ed), *Encyclopedia of Sleep and Dreaming*, New York: Macmillan, 1993.
Over four hundred articles. Emphasises scientific approaches.

Freud, S., *The Interpretation of Dreams*. J. Strachey (ed), *The Standard Edition of the Complete Psychological Works of Sigmund Freud*. Vols. 4-5. London: Hogarth Press, 1953. Originally published in 1900, a landmark in twentieth century literature.

Hall, J., *Jungian Dream Interpretation. A Handbook of Theory and Practice*. Toronto: Inner City Books, 1983.
An excellent introduction to Jungian dream psychology and interpretation.

Jung, C. G., *Dream Analysis. Notes of the Seminar Given in 1928-30*, Edited by W. McGuire, Bollingen Series XCIX. Princeton, NJ: Princeton University Press, 1984.
Gives a real flavour of Jung's own lecture style.

Jung, C. G., *Memories, Dreams, Reflections*, A. Jaffé (ed), New York: Random House, 1963.
An autobiography edited by his secretary that includes many of Jung's defining dreams.

Jung, C. G., *Dreams* (from the *Collected Works of C. G. Jung* Vols 4, 8, 12, 16) Translated by R. F. C. Hull (Princeton, NJ: Princeton University Press, 1974).
Brings together selected articles on dreams from the *Collected Works*.

Miller, P. C., *Dreams in Late Antiquity. Studies in the Imagination of a Culture*, Princeton, NJ: Princeton University Press, 1994.
A scholarly work on dream theory in early Christianity and its roots in ancient Western philosophy.

Sanford, J. *Dreams: God's Forgotten Language*, New York: J. B. Lippincott, 1968.
A classic introduction to Jungian-Christian dream analysis.

Taylor, J., *Dream Work. Techniques for Discovering the Creative Power in Dreams*, Ramsey, NJ: Paulist, 1983.
An introduction to dreamwork, with reference to dream-group techniques.

Vedfelt, O., *The Dimensions of Dreams*, New York: Fromm International, 1999.
A good overview of oneirology in all its aspects.

Glossary

Anima/Animus The feminine principle in a man, the masculine in a woman.

Archetypes Universally inherited ways in which humans understand, interpret and respond to the world. The basic content of religions and mythologies, they also determine some dreams.

Collective unconscious A hidden layer of the personality, common to humanity, which contains the archetypes.

Compensation A natural process aimed at establishing or maintaining balance within the psyche.

Complexes Ideas or images that carry an emotional charge for an individual, usually negative.

Conscious/consciousness That part of the psyche which is aware of a person's self, environment and mental activity and which to a certain extent determines thoughts and actions. Waking experience.

Divination The practice of discovering future events or unknown things through supernatural powers.

Dreamwork Dream analysis and interpretation. For Freud, the psychological mechanisms by which unconscious contents are translated into a dream narrative and its interpretation.

Ego The centre of personal consciousness.

Incubation Ancient religious ritual for seeking out divine contact in sleep.

Latent Qualities or potentials that are not obvious or revealed. Unconscious.

Manifest Qualities or potentials that are easily noticed or perceived. Conscious.

Neurobiology The branch of biology concerned with the structure and function of the cells of the nervous system.

Non-REM Non-Rapid Eye Movement sleep or inactive sleep. The 80% of sleep during which there is an absence of proper dreaming.

Numinous An experience of awe and wonder, imposed on a person, and associated with the presence of God.

Objective Existing independently of perception. A material item of the outside world as opposed to the image formed by an individual.

Oneirology The study of dreams. From the Greek, *onar* (dream), and *logos* (rational discourse).

Oneiric Pertaining to a dream.

Persona The role which the ego adopts in public.

Personal unconscious A layer of the psyche made up of forgotten, repressed or subliminal perceptions. Contains the complexes.

Physiology Branch of science concerned with the functioning of living organs.

Precognition The alleged ability to foresee future events.

Projection The perception of a personal quality in another person or object.

Projection The process whereby an unconscious item is attributed to a dream character or an object external to the psyche.

Psyche The totality of all psychological processes both conscious and unconscious that exist in complicated interplay in the individual.

Psychic Pertaining to the psyche.

Psychology The scientific study of behaviour, its make-up and causes.

REM Rapid Eye Movement sleep or active sleep. The 20% of sleep generally associated with dreams.

Self The archetype which expresses God's indwelling presence.

Shadow Personification of the inferior side of the personality.

Spirituality The experience of God and the academic and personal disciplines consequent to that encounter.

Subjective The perception of reality based on an individual's understanding, emotions, attitudes, etc.

Symbol The best possible sign for something unknown and unknowable.

Transcendent Function The psychic ability to supersede and reconcile the conflict between the conscious and the unconscious.

Transpersonal That which is common to humanity collectively, generally by unconscious means. For example, the archetypes.

Unconscious All psychic phenomena that lack normal awareness. For example, sleeping experience.